250

KERYGMA IN CRISIS?

1962

LOYOLA PASTORAL SERIES

Kerygma
in
crisis?

ALFONSO M. NEBREDA, S.J.

LOYOLA UNIVERSITY PRESS

Chicago 1965

To

Father James Keller, M.M.
for his friendship
and in deep admiration
for the achievements
of his twenty Christopher years

Preface

Vatican Council II, drawing on the powerful forces of renewal which have been at work now for decades in the Church, has made us joyously aware of the wonderful dynamism of the nature and mission of the Church in the world. As Bishop Carter has pointed out, whereas previous Councils were primarily concerned with the definition or redefinition of truths, Vatican II's primary goal was to reestablish contact with the modern world, to examine and reopen human relationships between the Church and those outside her fold.

It is in this perspective of the mission of the Church that the present book intends to present an overview of the situation, problems, and possibilities of transmitting the Christian message.

Chapter 1 studies the core of the Church's mission, living faith. The East Asian Study Week on Mission Catechetics, held at Bangkok in 1962, brought into clear focus for the first time in the history of catechetics the three stages which normally characterize the journey of an adult to faith:

1 *Pre-evangelization*; that is, a stage of preparation for the kerygma which, taking man as he is and where he is, makes a human dialogue possible and awakens in him the sense of God, an indispensable element for opening his heart to the message. 2 *Evangelization* or *kerygma*; that is, the dynamic heralding of the substance of the Christian message, having as its goal personal conversion or initial acceptance of Christ as the Lord. 3 *Catechesis proper*, which leans on the conversion achieved by the previous stages, and systematically develops the message. Its goal is to initiate man into Christian life and build within him a Christian personality.

When so articulated with regard to living faith, the mission of the Church appears in a striking new light. It might be well to single out some major pastoral conclusions that flow from such a conception.

First, the whole idea of the church's "mission" gains in depth and universality. It ceases to be a mere geographical or juridical concept and begins to stand out as "the act by which the Church goes beyond the frontiers of her own life to bear witness to Christ among those who do not know him."

Second, the concept of faith also grows richer. It goes above and beyond the mere holding of certain truths of revelation and becomes a personal response to God's word. As such it involves the whole man. This recovery of the true nature of Christian faith seems to be one of the most outstanding and far-reaching features of today's pastoral renewal in the Church.

Third, a reappraisal of our whole pastoral approach is in order. For centuries our pastoral activity and our pastoral institutions have taken as their pattern Christians who were baptized as children. When faith is seen as a *personal* response to God, it is obvious we cannot grasp it in its dynamic and organic process by using as our subject of study those who were baptized as children and could not ratify personally the pledge and promises of the sacrament. Although theologically justified and numerically normal in Christian countries, those baptized in infancy cannot serve as the subject of our study. The standard is and should be the adult who knowingly and willingly presents himself to the Church and asks for baptism, which changes him from a son of man into a son of God.

Finally, an honest scrutiny of our adult Catholics is also in order. For, even if some of our apparent securities be shaken, we should bluntly ask ourselves: How many of our baptized people have been evangelized? How many have ratified the commitment to Christ which others made in their name at baptism? An authentic pastoral concern cannot overlook this fact. As long as our Christians have not digested the content, fruits, and attitudes of the three stages mentioned above—especially conversion and real acceptance of Christ as the living Lord of their destiny— we cannot speak of full-fledged adult Christians. Only at the end of the three stages described can an adult normally be considered ready to receive baptism, which as the "sacrament of faith" crowns and seals the whole process. Here lurks the danger which threatens to spoil in its roots the pastoral activity of the Church in so-called Christian countries. When our small children receive baptism, which in the normal case crowns and seals the process of faith, there is a strong temptation to assume that the process of becoming a Christian is complete. Nothing is further from the truth. Baptism, indeed, confers the virtue of faith which is a supernatural power of making an act of faith. But far from dispensing us from further work, this demands that we help our children toward an ever more personal and mature act of faith.

In spite of all the achievements of the kerygmatic renewal, there are still some who are reluctant to welcome the new spirit. How are we to explain this reluctance?

First, there seems to be a confessed or subconscious fear of departing from "tradition." That is why Chapter II tries to show where and how the main road of catechesis went astray. It demonstrates that the type of catechesis which most of us learned when we were children is an unfortunate and recent deviation from the true tradition of catechetics in the history of the Church. As a matter of fact, the kerygmatic renewal, far from attacking tradition, actually returns to tradition.

Second, their reluctances seem to stem from a basically sound intuition, the need for balance. Yet the fact remains that for centuries there has been an unbalanced emphasis on the doctrinal aspect of the message. Only recently has catechetics recovered the balance and given proper emphasis to the dynamic aspect of Christianity.

However, it must always be kept in mind that God's message is basically a challenge. God speaks to man and invites him to respond at the level of faith. But before man can respond, he must realize that he is challenged. In order that this realization be present the hearer must be predisposed and prepared before introducing him to God's message. Without this "pre-evangelization" a purely kerygmatic approach will lead only to an impasse.

The remaining chapters of the book deal with the problem, theological foundations, and the principles and pedagogy of pre-evangelization.

If the Church's main problem today is to reestablish a dialogue with the modern world, then the major difficulties and objectives of the Church's mission will be brought into clearer focus by a study of pre-evangelization. It is the necessary bridge to any authentic human dialogue with the unbeliever.

The reader will kindly excuse certain repetitions and traces of the spoken style which he may detect in these pages. Despite painstaking editing and the addition of references, this book reflects the lectures given by the author during the summer of 1963 at the Catholic University of America, at St. Mary's College, Kansas, at the Glen Ellyn Summer Biblical Institute, and especially at the Catechetical Crossroads at Grailville, Ohio. Substantially they reproduce the text first prepared by Eva Fleischner and partially reproduced in *The Bulletin*, Grailville.

The author is happy to pay a public tribute of gratitude to the Grail team, particularly to Eva Fleischner for her devoted and intelligent work without which this book would not have been possible.

He owes a word of thanks to all those who, in one way or another, were responsible for his coming to this country and making it one of the most enriching experiences of his missionary life. It is but a duty to mention with gratitude and affection at least the names of Fathers James Keller, M.M., Theodore Stone, Mark Link, S.J. and Monsignor John Scanlon.

The author is also especially honored to join the ranks of those contributing to the Loyola Pastoral Series recently initiated by Loyola University Press.

Alfonso M. Nebreda, s.j.

The Christophers
New York City

August 24, 1964

Contents

Preface, vii

one   Toward a living faith, 1

two   Dynamism of the Christian message, 21

three   Kerygma in crisis? 45

four   From kerygma to pre-evangelization, 65

five   Principles of pre-evangelization, 95

six   Pedagogy of pre-evangelization, 109

Index, 135

Toward a living faith

Today the idea of "foreign missions" is vanishing in favor of the idea of the "mission of the Church." The mission of the Church, to quote Father Le Guillou, French Dominican specialist in ecumenical problems, can be defined as "the act by which the Church goes beyond the frontiers of her own life to bear witness to Christ among those who do not know him. The essential intention is to lead from non-belief to belief."[1]

The mission of the Church

If we so define the mission of the Church, we realize immediately that we can no longer maintain a rigid distinction between missionary countries and Christian countries. Rather the idea of "mission" applies to the whole world. Such a concept of mission sheds new light on how to deal with the different cases we meet in transmitting the message or in imparting religious reeducation.

1   M. J. Le Guillou, *Mission et unité*. Paris 1961. I, 88.

Let us review breifly the various categories of people which the Church meets in her mission.

First of all, there are the many nonbelievers. Daily we meet people who do not believe, the pagan or neopagan whom we find in growing numbers, even in our Christian milieux.

Second, there are the fallen-away Catholics.

Third, there are the "baptized non-Christians."[2] These frequently make up much of our congregations and classrooms, even in so-called Christian countries. I do not refer here to fallen-away Catholics, but to the many people who come regularly to Mass and receive the sacraments, but who, in regard to their belief, do not yet realize that Christian faith is something quite different. This leads us to a necessary distinction between the level of the sacraments (these people have been validly baptized) and the level of personal faith.[3] As soon as man can act in a personal way, he should make a commitment, by which faith becomes a human reality for him. To lead a man to an adult conversion and true commitment to Christ is one of the greatest challenges facing our Catholic schools.

Lastly, there are the fervent Catholics. Even for these conversion remains a permanent dimension of Christian existence. Only in heaven will we rest. Until then we must try and try again because what we conquer today we may lose tomorrow. A huge no-man's land always exists in us to be conquered, subjected to the domain of faith; that is, to Christ.

In the light of this breakdown we can see why a missionary approach is not limited to so-called missionary countries on the fringe of Christian existence. On the contrary, it has a relevance at the very core of Christian existence.

Viewed from the missionary approach—namely, leading the person from nonbelief to belief—most of today's discoveries (not only in scientific theology, missiology, and the like, but especially in pastoral activity) seem to lead us to a newer, deeper, and more existential sense of faith. It is a return to the Church's early history, when emphasis was clearly on faith and on the word. St. Paul says plainly, "Faith then depends on hearing" (Romans 10:17). That is why, when we speak of faith, implicitly we mean preaching, transmitting the word.

The word and faith remain central to all the new discoveries today, or better to all our rediscoveries. In our Lord's missionary command faith comes first; "he who believes and is baptized" (Mark 16:16; Matthew 28:19). First faith, then baptism. St. Paul even says that he has been sent not to baptize but to evangelize; this is, to preach, confronting the hearer with faith (I Corinthians 1:17).

When the apostles realized that they could not perform all activities in the infant Church, they decided to remain servants of the word. Other matters could be managed by deacons and others. But this aspect of serving the faith—namely, serving the word in order to provoke faith—is the typical activity which the first missionaries, the apostles, considered their task (Acts 6:2-4).

Danger of sacramentalism

This situation prevailed almost until the time of Trent, the main emphasis always on faith. After Trent, however, a significant trend occurred, which we may take as a warning against too close ties with local or temporal situations. Catechesis must be adapted to the times, yet must not reflect too exclusively the one-sided emphasis of any given place or era.

What happened was this. The theologians and the catechists of the Counter Reformation combatted the reformer's negation of the core of the Church's sacramental activity so vehemently that a one-sided emphasis on the

2 See A. M. Henry, O.P., "Le Baptême des enfants des incroyants," *Parole et Mission* 6 (1963), 397-401.

3 *Ibid.*, pp. 408 ff.

sacraments developed. Because Protestants denied the sacraments, Catholic theologians—and later catechists also—stressed their objective efficacy.[4]

This aspect must be stressed. We cannot, however, accept such a one-sided emphasis for, as the Church's entire tradition shows, the sacraments are either "signs of faith" or they are nothing. Even worse than nothing, they may be simply magical formulas which mislead people.[5]

Let us be realistic. Although we are recovering a balance in seeing the sacraments within the context of faith, I still fear many Christians have a one-sided view of the sacraments. They look at them cut off from their meaningful and vital context; that it, from faith.[6]

Take, for instance, the case of a boy who is a very fervent Christian. He goes to confession every Saturday, receives Communion every Sunday. Now unfortunately today is Monday and he has committed a sin; but since he usually goes to Saturday confession he says, "Well, anyhow, I'll go next Saturday."

I ask you to analyze, through your own observations of people and their behavior, what happens to such a person. I am not trying to exaggerate or caricature the situation, but I fear that often, through inadequate understanding of the sacraments, people forget that the sacrament of penance must be seen in the context of faith. It is absurd to think that by going to confession next Saturday, without any thought of meeting Christ, a sort of magic miracle will happen.

I do not refer here to people who say to themselves, "Well, now I am in mortal sin, I might as well go on sinning. Since I must go to confession next Saturday, I will confess four sins instead of three, that's all." This would be an extreme case; I do not wish to go so far.

I imagine instead the case of a typical Catholic. No one has taught this boy that what is more important than the sacraments, from a psychological viewpoint and therefore from the viewpoint of his attitude, is the way he looks at the sacraments.[7] If he looks at the sacraments as a personal meeting with Christ, all is well. But if he is aware that he can meet Christ in the sacraments, why is he not aware that Christ is someone living today? Why must he wait for Saturday to apologize to this living Christ? Obviously he disregards or misunderstands many elements here: the very concept of contrition, of grace, which is essentially restoration of a friendship that has been broken. To a person such as I have described a sacrament is a static or purely material thing.

When Saturday finally comes he goes to Church. (He has been uncomfortable all week, and has never thought he could and should get rid of that sin at once and not wait for confession.) He kneels down and prepares his confession. Allow me to guess this boy's main concern. Is it to prepare for what is most important—meeting Christ and telling him personally that he is sorry? That would be a real encounter. Or is it simply taking all precautions to perform a rite, putting the main emphasis on correct external performance? If that is true, we should not be astonished when a mature professional man of fifty confesses in the same words a child uses—the same words he has used since his second-grade teacher prepared him for his first confession.

Let us return to the boy. When he comes out of church a sister or priest says to me: "Wonderful, isn't it? You can almost see in his eyes the brightening effects of the grace

4 For a brief exposition of the Tridentine sacramentology too determined by polemical concern see Matthew J. O'Connell, "The Sacraments in Theology Today," *Thought* 36 (1961), 40-58, especially pp. 41-44.

5 P. Fransen, S.J., *Faith and the Sacraments*. London 1958. See also his "Sacraments, Signs of Faith," *Worship* 37 (1962), 31-49.

6 A. M. Henry, O.P., "Le Baptême des enfants des incroyants," *Parole et Mission* 6 (1963), 404-18; also "La pastorale missionaire

auprès des baptisés," *Parole et Mission* 5 (1962), 438 ff.

7 For the present-day insistence on the *opus operantis* in the reception of the sacraments, see the following: H. Schillebeeckx, *De sacramentale Heilseconomie*. Antwerp 1952. L. Villette, *Foi et Sacrement*. Paris 1959. See also K. Rahner, "Personale und sakramentale Frömmigkeit"; in *Schriften zur Theologie* Einsiedeln 1954. II, 115-41. Summarized in *Theology Digest* III (1955), 93-98.

of the sacrament!" When I hear something like this I am tempted to shout "Nonsense!" What is the grace of the sacrament here? It is exactly what any normal citizen feels when he has paid a fine or his income tax. "Now everything is all right. I have paid!" What is the *penance* in the sacrament of penance for many Christians? For a number of people penance means going to church and being ready to work off a fine or receive a reprimand from the priest. This shows a lack of understanding of the sacrament.

I fear this kind of psychology is still quite prevalent. For many people the whole sacramental world is meaningless.[8] Can you imagine two persons who call themselves friends but never speak to each other? We would conclude either that they are not friends or that something is wrong with them. Yet there are Christians who look upon confession as nothing more than some "thing" that "puts them in order." "Now I am all right!" That is why they come to confession and say: "Against the first commandment, nothing . . . Against the second commandment, nothing . . . Against the third . . ." I say to them, "Do you think Christianity is something negative?" Their main concern of Christian existence is apparently security, being "all right." We are not "all right." The first Christians had a wonderful awareness of the nothingness, the sinfulness of man. And by "man" I mean here Christian. St. John even says: "If we say that we have not sinned, we make him [God] a liar" (I John 1:10). Why? What would be the sense of God's sending his own Son to *save* us if we had no sin and did not need salvation? A Christian is not "in order"; he is "in Christ." The idea of morality held by too many Christians is that the commandments oblige one like a sort of law-enforcement agent. This conception denies the essence of Christian morality, which is liberation from any law, replacing it by the Spirit of Christ in the atmosphere of faith.[9] For St. Paul "in Christ" is at the same time the realm of faith and the realm of morality. Everything is perfectly unified there.[10]

Let us illustrate. A man who lived in the time of George Washington comes back to life again. He enters an office and sees a girl talking on the phone. He stares at her in astonishment and finally says, "This girl must be crazy. She's talking to herself!" What is the difference between talking to oneself like a madman and talking over the phone? In the second case there is someone to answer the call. Something similar to the above can happen when one performs a sacred rite. For example, baptizing a dying child in front of a whole family of nonbelievers. I did this in Japan recently. You are aware in such a situation that you are a strange sight to the onlookers. Everyone stares at you. You pour water on the head of the child and you know this has a wonderful—literally a divine—meaning and effect. Everyone standing around you has seen the same action, but they say, "What does this mean?" What is it that makes you see in this action something that the nonbeliever does not see? Faith. It is only in the light of faith that the whole sacramental reality of the Church— salvation history prolonged and actualized for me—takes on life and meaning.[11] Faith gives intelligibility to the sacraments and is nurtured and deepened by them.

Here we must dispel a common misunderstanding. Many people seem to think that baptism gives faith because the ritual of baptism begins with the priest's question "What do you ask of the Church of God?" and the answer "Faith." They think that in baptism you receive faith. Can you imagine an adult not believing—at least with that *initium fidei* of which the Council of Orange (Arausica)

8 See A. M. Henry, "Le Baptême des enfants des incroyants," *Parole et Mission* 6 (1963), 402.
9 See S. Lyonnet, "Liberty and Law," *Theology Digest* XI (1963), 12-18.
10 I highly recommend the book of P. A. Liégé, O.P., *What Is Christian Life?* New York 1961.

11 See Bernard Cooke, S.J., "The Sacraments as the Continuing Acts of Christ," *Proceedings of the Catholic Theological Society of America* 16 (1961), 43-68.

speaks—and receiving the graces of the sacrament? In this case God would be acting in a most unlikely way, thrusting himself upon man, forcing his gifts upon someone who did not want to receive them. That is why faith must precede the sacrament of baptism if the sacrament is to have any meaning. The Church's entire tradition is most emphatic on this point.[12] I do not speak here of the *habit* of faith. I mean faith as the psychological attitude which precedes baptism.

A comprehensive initial faith is essential. The fact that we have this confusion in the ritual shows the need for reform. The recent permission granted by Rome to use the separate stages for the administration of baptism[13] is a welcome and encouraging sign. In our actual baptismal ritual we have a formula that combines both the ritual of baptism proper and the ritual used in the first centuries for introduction to the catechumenate.[14] One enters the catechumenate precisely with the understanding that he asks for faith and is already praying for faith.

Recovery of a richer concept of faith

Another important aspect of the missionary point of view is the recovery of a broader, all-embracing idea of faith. During the Reformation the Protestants attacked faith both from the viewpoint of *content* (orthodoxy) and *profession*. As a result it became necessary to stress the outward profession that one was Catholic. It was normal for men such as Bellarmine to stress in their catechesis on faith just these two points: faith as content and faith as profession. Had Catholics kept the other two aspects of faith along with these, all would have been well. But they forgot, practically speaking, to stress the other equally necessary elements: faith as commitment and faith as trust. Protestants had stressed these one-sidedly, and Catholic theologians and catechists went to the other extreme. Consequently, for at least two centuries (and I fear still today), faith has meant simply "orthodoxy."

We must not forget that man cannot nourish his spiritual life with orthodoxy alone.[15] The aim of catechesis can never be simply to transmit correct information. Too often our emphasis in teaching is on correctness alone, with the result that sometimes we go overboard. Instead of orthodoxy we venerate *orthology*, the science of speaking correctly. We insist not only on thinking correctly but on speaking correctly! But there is more to Christianity than this. There must also, and above all, be correct practice, correct life, for faith *is* life.

For the last two centuries in catechetics this has practically been forgotten. It is remarkable that in the last thirty years we seem to have almost changed roles with Protestant theologians. Originally they so stressed the aspect of trust and commitment that we went to the other extreme and insisted one-sidedly on objectivity, correctness, orthodoxy. Today developments in Catholic theology are leading us to stress, even more forcefully than the Protestants, the personal aspect of faith. Take, for instance, J. Mouroux's books,[16] or the tract of Father J. Alfaro of the Gregorian,[17] or R. Aubert's very fundamental book.[18] These works insist so much on the personal, existential trust sense of faith that they seem to have swung

12 See J. Mouroux, *Christian Experience*. New York 1954. pp. 48-60. I purposely limit myself to the baptism of adults. The infant baptism follows another line, well justified by sound theological principles; but for all its numerical normality, this cannot be considered as the type when we study things from the angle of faith.

13 *Acta Apostolicae Sedis* 54 (1962), 310-15. See also P. M. Gy, "Le nouveau rite du baptême des adultes," *Maison-Dieu* 7 (1962), 15-27 and F. Antonelli, *Costituzione Conciliare sulla Sacra Liturgia*, edited by R. Falsini. Rome 1964. pp. 253-54.

14 See A. Stenzel, *Die Taufe*, Innsbruck 1958. T. Maertens, *Histoire et Pastorale du catéchuménat et du baptême*. Bruges 1962.

15 Professor F. X. Arnold has described in a masterly fashion both the historical deviation and the balanced Christian view of faith as *fides quae* and *fides qua* at the same time. See, among others: *Dienst am Glauben*. Freiburg 1948. pp. 24 ff. *Glaubensverkündigung und Glaubensgemeinschaft*. Düsseldorf 1955. Chapters 1 and 2. "The Act of Faith, a Personal Commitment," *Lumen Vitae* V (1950), 251-56. "Faith as Assent and Commitment," *Lumen Vitae* XI (1956), 571-82.

16 *I Believe*. New York 1960. *From Baptism to the Act of Faith*. Boston 1963.

17 *Adnotationes in tractatum de virtutibus*. Rome 1959. See also "Persona y Gracia," *Gregorianum* 41 (1960), 5-29 and "Fides in Terminologia Biblica," *Gregorianum* 42 (1961), 463-505.

18 *Le problème de l'acte de foi*. Louvain 1958.

over to the Protestant view. The Protestants, on the other hand, are beginning to stress more than ever today the objectivity of faith, without which faith cannot be distinguished from superstition. This is a healthy sign, one of greater balance.

Today, thank God, we are returning to the best theological tradition of St. Augustine and St. Thomas, to the traditional formula which explained faith as *credere Deum, credere Deo,* and *credere in Deum. Credere Deum* means to believe God as the object, the target of our thinking (provided we do not forget that God is never an object but a Person). It is important to note St. Thomas' emphasis on this point, "Faith never stops at the statement but goes beyond the statement to the reality explained in it."[19] We find the same idea in Newman, who emphasized the need to stress real assent above notional assent. This is an important point for all catechesis.

We often make wonderful statements about the faith, but do we ask ourselves what they mean to children? "I believe in the Incarnation." "I do not believe in the Incarnation!" What is *Incarnation?* It is a word. I remember how one of our theology professors in Spain said, when he discussed "the Incarnate Word" (in Spanish, "Verbo encarnado"): "If you use these words in a village, the villagers may think you are talking about one of those gunmen, El Verbo, a bandit." *Encarnado* in Spanish means "red"—so you have "the Red Bandit." These terms are relics of medieval times when it was considered fine to choose the most abstract of abstractions. Today we no longer have this mentality. Why go on speaking about the Trinity, the Incarnation, the Redemption? These are words; abstractions that do not exist. I believe in the Father. I believe in Jesus. I believe in the Son. I believe in the Holy Spirit. These are personal realities. All this may seem mere external detail, but unless we strive toward such purification, our children will always remain blissfully ignorant of the reality underlying these abstractions.

When I say "Credo Deum" I mean I believe God as *someone*. I mean this not merely as an assent to a truth but essentially as an adherence to a person—an adherence from within. This, precisely, is faith; and such an assent implies the whole activity of the Holy Spirit leading us to a new knowledge.

The second aspect is *credere Deo*, which means to believe God. When we say to a person, "I believe you," it is different from saying, "I believe that someone has said that" or "I believe a truth." "I believe you" implies a total context where the person as such is involved. This is the second aspect of faith which must be stressed. You tell God, "I believe you. I do not need extra reports or proofs—I believe you." When a girl tells a boy, "I believe you," the deepest level of personal relation is involved. To say "I believe you" to God means to accept God as the highest witness, who gives us the only type of certainty needed in Christianity. For the certitude of our faith comes, not from evidence of a truth, but from credibility of a Person.[20]

When I say *credere in Deum* I refer to a new dynamism by which God is simultaneously the highest truth, the highest value, and above all the highest happiness. I do not need to make distinctions. I know that through my self-commitment and self-involvement as a person, Christ—and God in Christ—is assuring me of my highest happiness and my highest truth.[21]

These correct ideas are gradually permeating the whole field of catechetics. If we study the evolution of catechetics in the last fifty years from the angle of faith (the missionary viewpoint of leading a man from unbelief to

19 "Fides non terminatur ad enuntiabile sed ad rem." *Summa Theologica* II IIae q. 1, 2, 2m.
20 See the two articles by F. X. Arnold published in *Lumen Vitae* V (1950), 251-56 and XI (1956), 571-82.

21 For the designative usage of *credere in* in Christian Latin see Christine Mohrman, *Études sur le latin des Chrétiens*. Rome 1958. pp. 195-203.

belief), we recognize a shift of emphasis from the *object* of belief (a stress on information, instruction, teaching) to the *subject*. How does faith affect me as believer, my mentality as well as my behavior? How do I become a Christian person? This is what Father Van Caster calls the "stage of formation," the stage when Christian values begin to form and build a Christian personality.[22]

Finally, emphasis in recent years has shifted to *interpersonal relationships*. God's revelation is studied in a more personal light; man's answer in faith is also personalized. Thus faith is stressed as a personal commitment.

As Father Van Caster points out, the correct order is usually assumed to be a chronological one. First inform your students, give them correct information about God. Then gradually this information will produce a sort of formation. The students will change their personalities, begin to think as Christians, and behave somewhat like Christians. Then—only then at the peak of this process— will come the third state: initiation into the mystery of God, communion with God.[23]

Actually, the contrary is true. Unless we start at the very beginning with the aspect of initiation—leading our students to meet God, to experience of God as *Someone* —even the level of formation will not be achieved nor will information be transmitted correctly.

The personalist approach To help us understand this personalist approach, let us draw upon current developments in phenomenology, existential philosophy, and psychology. These will help us penetrate to the reality of person and, in so doing, lead us to Christian reality. This personalistic approach seems to be a convergent trend in many different milieux today— for Catholics like Gabriel Marcel, for a man like Martin Buber, who is a Jew, for a Protestant like Paul Tillich, for a man like Shestov, a Russian Orthodox. All these men realize that we are entering an era in which—because of the depersonalizing process that confronts us daily—a catastrophe will befall us unless we react and realize more deeply the uniqueness of the *personal* life.

This trend provides ideal background for a deeper understanding of the meaning of faith. We ordinarily assume that "knowledge" is one simple reality in all cases. This is not correct. Let me illustrate. It is one thing to know *something* and quite a different thing to know *someone*. Unless we realize this, we will continue day after day, even as good Catholics, to apply to persons the same categories we apply to objects, seeing in people not their personal features but only their functions. Mr. So and So, what is he? A professor at the university. A "professor" is a title that reduces him to a number, a figure. The fact of the matter is that he is *Mr. So and So*—unique. Or we speak about the "policeman," the "postman," and so on. We are simply trying to satisfy our abstractions, our depersonalizing instinct.

We must begin by emphasizing strongly what is unique. In all nature we shall not find two things the same. Any scientist will tell you that not even two leaves on a tree are alike. This applies still more to persons. If we could only see into the hearts of twins and see how they react to things and persons, we would be astonished that people could confuse them. Each is totally different. This is the mark, the trademark of God. God seems to throw away his mold every time he creates anything, especially when he creates a human being.

I am often asked, "How can you prove that God loves me personally?" I say, "Either God loves *you*, or he does not love at all." For the only reality that exists is you and you and you. We speak of "men," "women," "boys,"

22 Marcel Van Caster, S.J., "Teaching, Formation and Initiation," *Lumen Vitae* XVI (1961), 607-16.

23 See the beautiful article of F. Taymans d'Eypernon, S.J., "Faith, Man's Communion with God," *Lumen Vitae* IX (1954), 182-93.

"girls," but these concepts are our inventions. We are proud of our so-called universal concepts and devote numerous philosophical theses to them. We are proud of this and rightly so, if we compare ourselves to a dog. But I am convinced that when God looks at us, at our way of reasoning and abstracting, he must be highly amused. We are forced to kill things in order to feed them into the pigeon holes of our brains. We speak about "the trees." What is "the tree"? In order to put an object at the level of our grasping and handling we build up a universal concept and apply it to everything. Actually it no longer fits anything adequately because, after all, this tree is this tree, and that tree is that tree. All reality is unique; persons especially are unique. For our comfort we have invented concepts that seem to work. In this we resemble a biologist who in order to analyze life dissects it. In order to analyze life he kills it. In a similar way we deal with things and persons.

How, then, is it possible to *know* a person? First of all, you cannot truly express yourself in words or concepts because you are unique. If your words did truly express you, you would be inventing words every day until finally no one would understand you. You would have to invent your own vocabulary because your experience, if sufficiently analyzed, is unique. The fact is that great personalities in moments of deep personal consciousness actually do invent expressions—poetry. We normal human beings, however, must resign ourselves to our situation. Yet when we feel deep sorrow or joy, we realize that our words cannot express what we feel, and we retreat into silence. This is a normal human experience. The fact is that words simply cannot express accurately the uniqueness we feel in ourselves.

The same communication problem is also true of our concepts which, as we saw, are built up by abstractions, by draining off, as it were, the common features of a uniquely existing reality.

How then is a person known? Only through a revelation of himself. We forget this when we talk about God. What is the meaning of revelation? It means that a person comes out of himself, makes himself understood, shows himself. You cannot know someone unless he, out of love, manifests his intimacy. If a boy goes somewhere where he is unknown and, if he decides not to communicate with anyone, he will remain unknown. You can look at a hundred pictures of him but will not know him unless he goes out of himself and says, "I am so and so."

Another very important point that applies also to God is that we are known more by indirect means—the tone of our voice, the look in our eyes, a gesture, silence—than simply by words. This is true because, as we said, words somehow kill the unique quality of our self-expression.

What then is the way to know a person? Not through words or mere concepts, but though a sort of sixth sense, an intuition,[24] a kind of sympathy, a feeling with the other. Max Scheler, in his classic work *Wesen und Formen der Sympathie*, gives a wealth of insights into this important point.[25]

Imagine that you have heard many things about a person but have never met him. Do you know that person? No. You know *about* him. But unless you meet him you will not know *him*. By "meeting a person" I do not mean, of course, being merely physically present to him. You can meet him as if he were a tree, and your impression will be a wrong one. I mean personal meeting, what I call "intuition," "sympathy," a sort of connatural knowledge which is already understanding and therefore love.

24 In "The Primacy of Intuition," *Thought* 37 (1962), 57-73, Gerald A. McCool reviews in a penetrating way new trends in Catholic thought concerning intuition. He has in mind works of A. Brunner, Balthasar, K. Rahner, but especially the important thesis of C. Cirne-Lima, *Der personale Glaube*. Innsbruck 1959. See also A. H. Maltha, O.P., *Die neue Theologie*. Munich 1960. Maltha stresses the intuitive emphasis as the first characteristics of the contemporary renewal in theology.

25 Bonn 1923. English translation by P. Heath under the title *The Nature of Sympathy*. New Haven 1954.

Father de Letter offers an excellent analysis of the point discussed here.[26] Encounter is the meeting of persons in an "I—Thou" relationship on the level of mutual understanding and love. Not purely conceptual knowledge, however, but a sort of general *synthetic* intuition which results not by reasoning, but by "seeing" from the ensemble of many partial experiences and ideas. Knowledge of a person cannot be expressed in a concept which, of its very nature, refers to a quality or form and does not of itself represent a *subject*. Person involves relation and opposition to the other. Only by intuition do we know a relation. The intuition reaches the person from the light of this synthetic view. Meeting is essentially the conscious living of the "I—Thou" relationship.

*From
love to
knowledge*

When we enter the realm of the personal, it is not true to say that knowledge produces understanding and love. Rather the contrary is true. Love alone produces understanding and, therefore, true knowledge. This point is essential for the whole of catechesis. Unless we approach a person with a well-disposed attitude, we shall miss the point. We often say, "His mother is blind" because she is convinced that her son, considered by others a criminal, is at heart really good. No, the blindness is ours. She alone has eyes to see the person. We approach him with cold objectivity, actually the very opposite of true objectivity. We are so objective that we have killed the very feature of personal knowledge and reduced the person to a thing.

We must realize that people agree to reveal themselves only out of love. The moment we enter into contact with another person in an attitude that is not creating, permeating, breathing love in a sort of radiation, the other person instinctively feels ill at ease. He will instinctively react by putting on a mask, so that we cannot really know him. We will go home and say, "Of course I know that person"; but all who know him will say, "You missed the point." We have seen a caricature of him because we have seen only the facade and regarded it as the person. Almost without realizing it this person has retreated into himself, refusing to open and reveal himself to us, so that even with the best intention we cannot see and know him as he is.

A striking incident from my life in Japan may help to illustrate. Some years ago I visited a Zen-Buddhist temple about eighty miles south of Tokyo. While there I had a long, interesting conversation with a Buddhist monk. He was a Zen Buddhist, a member of what is probably the most important religious group of Japan's entire history. Even today they maintain a high standard. Outstanding religious personalities are found among them. This seventy-five-year-old master of novices was a wonderful person. We talked almost three hours while he told me many interesting things about their religious thought and practice. After three hours I made the big "mistake." I asked him: "You have been master of novices almost forty years. I should like to know how you manage to put across to your novices these religious experiences? How can you transmit a personal experience in words?" The old monk smiled and began to compliment me. (Japanese are extremely polite, and you should be aware of this when they compliment you.) "For three hours now I was really pleased to see how wonderfully well you speak our language. If I had been blind, I would have said that you are not a foreigner, but Japanese. And yet . . ." Then he came to the real point, "yet this question of yours, even if I had been blind, would have told me that you are not Japanese after all." To my question on how to transmit personal experience, he answered: "Only by two personalities, so to say, 'rubbing each other.' The one who is

26 "The Encounter with God," *Thought* 36 (1961), 5-24.

somehow receptive will get your message. If he is not receptive, you had better give up. Wait for maturity. Until then it is hopeless."

For the first time in my life, perhaps, I understood, almost instinctively, something of the whole mentality of the Old and the New Testament, especially of St. John when he speaks of "knowing." In the classical text, John 17, our Lord himself gives us the ideal of Christian life, which is of course the ideal, the purpose of the whole transmission of the message, especially in catechesis. The Lord himself says, "Now this is everlasting life that they may know thee, the only true God, and him whom thou hast sent, Jesus Christ" (John 17:3). I am afraid that most of us miss the point when we think about knowing God. Yet it is Christ himself who says that life everlasting in heaven and the life of grace and faith here below (which are identical in that we already possess the same divine life that will be ours in fullness when the veil of faith is removed) consist in knowing God, knowing Christ. This knowledge of God, however, is not an activity of our intellect alone, as we with a Western mentality are inclined to believe![27]

To know a person is to meet him fully at that point where not only the mind, but especially the heart decides. Father de la Taille, one of the greater theologians of this century, could write: "The light of faith, although residing in the mind, does not enter man through the mind; but through the heart. There is its door of entry, the passage through which God pours this light more or less abundantly, more or less alive, according as love itself lives in us beyond any other affection, or, on the contrary, as self-love dominates over or oppresses love of God."[28]

Newman also realized that the approach to faith is not intellectual but essentially moral, a problem therefore of the heart. But this is not in the sense in which classical apologetics stresses that those who sin and do not leave their sinful state will not see God, following our Lord's words that only "the clean of heart shall see God." It is not in this obvious, often superficially understood sense, but in the true sense that you can never understand a value unless you are already connaturally open to it. You will never understand justice unless you love it. You will never really understand peace unless you love it. This is a practical point for us today. Many Catholics do not have the proper attitude toward peace, precisely because they are breathing an atmosphere where real peace is mere theory. They have a hierarchy of values in which peace is secondary. What applies to values applies even more directly to persons.

Let me give an example. Take a great man like Einstein or some great poet with many followers and students. Imagine a brilliant disciple of Einstein, who has written many books about him and knows his theories in detail. Who knows Einstein better as a person, as Einstein? Is it this brilliant student or is it Einstein's wife? Surely his wife. The disciple knows a thousand times more about Einstein, of course; but knowing him as a person is different from knowing his theories. Knowing him as a person requires insight, love, and therefore humility. This supposes that we already have an attitude of going out, willingness to follow as did Abraham, our father in the faith. This going out of ourselves is the only way to approach someone as a person and to try to understand him as he is.

Unless the approach of faith begins with a total meeting with God, considering God as Someone—through initiation, communion, encounter—not only will formation not be achieved in a true Catholic sense, but even the process of information, which we call instruction, will never be truly Christian.

27 See Thomas Barrosse, C.S.C., "The Relationship of Love to Faith in St. John," *Theological Studies* 18 (1957), 538-59.

28 M. de la Taille, S.J., "L'oraison contemplative," *Recherches de Science religieuse* 9 (1919), 279.

We may conclude, therefore, that the missionary approach forcefully centers the Church's entire research and practical concern on "faith as the core of her mission." Hence it focusses the attention of our catechetical movement where it belongs, on essentials.[29] For "this is everlasting life, that they may know thee, the only true God, and him whom thou has sent, Jesus Christ."

---

29 For an appreciation of the importance of this approach in the field of catechetics see A. M. Nebreda, S.J., "Living Faith: Major Concern of Religious Education"; in *Pastoral Catechetics*, edited by J. Hofinger and T. Stone. New York 1964. pp. 121-43.

Chapter two *Dynamism*
of the
Christian message

A major challenge for the church today is the growth of
a worldwide technological civilization.[1] The most diverse
cultures are in the process of being unified to such an
extent that we wonder what will be the specific problems
of a country like Japan, or India, twenty years from now.
I may be biased by my own Japanese experience, but I
fear that what is happening in Japan today will soon be
the common lot of the whole world.

The
challenge
of our It is as if the dreams of Auguste Comte, father of positiv-
technological ism in the last century, had begun to materialize. His
civilization theory points out three stages in human civilization.[2]

First comes the theological stage, where man attributes
everything he fails to understand to hidden powers, to

1 See A. Desqueyrat, *Le civilisé peut-il croire?*
Bruges 1963.

2 See Henri de Iubac, S.J., *Le drame de l'hu-*
manisme athée. Sixth edition, Paris 1959. Part II,
especially pp. 141-49.

God. Thus if he hears thunder, he will speak of the god of thunder, and so forth. Then when man becomes more sophisticated, he enters the realm of metaphysics. This is the metaphysical or philosophical stage, where theories and systems take the place of God. Thirdly, according to Comte, we reach the positivistic era, where science either explains everything or will explain everything.

I believe that if Comte were alive today, he would be astonished to see how strong this conviction is among many people. This is especially so among Japanese students and educated people in general. As a result Japanese intellectuals reject religion in the name of reason, whereas common people reject reason in the name of religion.[3] The final outcome is that both groups discredit religion as such. This situation makes us wonder whether in the near future there will be any room for true religion at all.

Paradoxically, together with this situation there are thousands of pseudoreligions (as we already have them in Japan) in addition to total agnosticism and atheism. Millions of people join the so-called "new religions" or new sects. After the war there were several hundred new religions in Japan—the "religion of electricity," the "religion of the dance," "perfect-freedom religion," and so forth.[4] These new religions have one thing in common: such an absurd syncretism that religion is utterly discredited in the eyes of most normal and sensible people.

I fear this will be the picture of the technological civilization which is conquering the entire world.[5] When I passed through India in the fall of 1962, I was very cautious in my judgment because I knew that the religious situation there is quite different from that in Japan. And yet, professors in several Indian colleges told me over and over again: "The situation that exists already in Japan we are now experiencing here with our elite. Those who go to America and Europe for further study return so sophisticated that religion is meaningless to them. Eventually, when they get old, they return to some type of religious practice from a sort of nostalgia; but religion itself means nothing to them."

This problem, I believe, presents a great opportunity for the Church today. And I do not think that I am a dreamer. But first we must purify Christianity. We must cut away what is accidental to our faith and concentrate on its essentials—the very core. If we can free our faith of the cultural and historical accretions that do not belong to its essence, we will be able to give this technological civilization exactly what it yearns for. Despite the great difficulties it carries to the faith, this technological civilization also brings wonderful positive elements.[6] To give but one example, no one can deny that true scientists are very close to the sense of mystery. They are so conscious of their own limitations that they easily develop genuine religious attitudes. If we compare the evolution of Jean Rostand's views, as found in the books he wrote around 1930 with his recent books, we are amazed at the change. His earlier writings show an obvious contempt for religion; not so with those toward the end of his life. In 1961, when an Italian scientist started laboratory experiments on the procreative activity of man, it was Jean Rostand who wrote the most scathing indictment of these proceedings: "If we continue along these lines, we will soon achieve the dehumanization of the whole of mankind."

The technological civilization in itself has nothing that cannot be Christianized, provided we give scientists something that they can understand.[7] Our big task is, therefore,

3 See J. Roggendorf, S.J., "The Place of Religion in Modern Japan," Japan Quarterly 5 (1958), 21-29.
4 H. van Straelen, and Clark Offner, Modern Japanese Religions. Tokyo 1962. R. Hammer, Japan's Religious Ferment. New York 1962. pp. 135-44.
5 For a brighter outlook on the task confronting Christianity vis-a-vis the technological civilization, see J. Daniélou, S.J., The Scandal of Truth. Baltimore 1962. pp. 115-28.
6 See J. Loew and G. M. M. Cottier, Dynamisme de la foi et incroyance. Paris 1963.
7 See L'Athéisme, tentation du monde, reveil des chrétiens. Paris 1963.

one of purification. The big question is, however, how can we begin this process of purification?

If we look at the presentation of God's message by the early Church, we find some helpful insights as to how we could and should proceed today. First of all, we must show men that Christianity is not just another religion, another morality, another philosophy, another conception of life. It is something unique. But how can we present the uniqueness, the originality of the Christian message? This is the biggest challenge that faces the Church and her mission today.

What is the core of Christianity? It is, simply, the mystery of Christ as St. Paul and almost every book in the New Testament reveals.[8] Bishop Emmett Carter gives an accurate presentation of the main features of Christianity. The five propositions which he sets down are a beautiful expression of the elements that enter into the mystery of Christ and encompass the characteristics of the kerygmatic renewal.[9] By "mystery," of course, we do not mean simply something that we do not fully understand. It is not just a puzzle, a riddle, a problem. Gabriel Marcel has made classic the distinction between "problem" and "mystery." A problem is something objective, reified; one is always looking for a solution to it in a detached, depersonalized way. A mystery, on the contrary, is something which engages and involves the whole person. It must be accepted personally and approached with respect and love.[10] This is what we call the mystery of Christ.[11] We should not emphasize the element of not understanding, not being able to understand. On the contrary, we should stress that it is the mystery, the plan, of a Person—a wonderful Person, who out of love has decided to leave his own intimacy and manifest himself to us. The Person is God the Father who, in Christ, through his Spirit, has called us to share his own life.

The Old and New Testament, the Church, the liturgy, all the essential elements of our faith teach that God the Father has called us to himself through his Son. My students in Japan were very happy to learn that God is Father.[12] This was the beginning of a real revelation for them, because they are orphans. We also are orphans. More than ever we need to conquer this loneliness which seems to be a by-product of our "wonderful" era. For what we need and crave for is not a kind of material, objective presence, but a presence made of spirit, of understanding, of love.[13] Now when we say that God is Father we are merely stressing what Harnack considered the main revelation of Christ. For Harnack, Christianity's great witness was directed to the fatherhood of God. We may analyze any other religion, and we shall not find anything really comparable to the Christian concept of the fatherhood of God. We must understand it correctly, however. God is Father, not in a paternalistic or grandfatherly way, treating the child almost as a kind of pet. He is a real father who, in his Son, through his Spirit, invites us to live his own life. That is why the whole teaching of the Church Fathers can be summed up in the expression *filii in Filio*: he made us "children in his Son."[14] He is not a God who out of a certain benevolence decided to sign a paper and say, "From now on we are going to consider these poor people as our own." No. As St. John

8 See, for instance, D. Grasso, S.J., "The Core of Missionary Preaching"; in *Teaching All Nations. A Symposium on Modern Catechetics*, edited by J. Hofinger. New York 1961. (Pages 39-58 in the London edition.)

9 G. Emmett Carter, "Head and Heart," *America* 109 (1963), 40-43.

10 Jean-Pierre Bagot, *Connaissance et Amour, Essai sur la philosophie de Gabriel Marcel*. Paris 1958. pp. 178 ff.

11 See the article by D. Deden which remains a classic, "Le Mystère Paulinien," *Ephemerides Theologicae Lovanienses* 13 (1936), 403-42. See also J. A. Jungmann, S.J., "Theology and Kerygmatic Teaching," *Lumen Vitae* V (1950), 258-63 and A. Haman, *Le Mystère de Salut*. Paris 1954.

12 See R. Guelluy, *Vie de Foi et tâches terrestres*. Tournai 1961. Especially the first chapter, "La portée religieuse du dogme de la création," pp. 13-29.

13 See how the Bangkok Study Week stressed the importance of this point in pre-evangelization. A. M. Nebreda, S.J., "East Asian Study Week on Mission Catechetics," *Lumen Vitae* XVII (1962), 725.

14 See Emile Mersch, S.J., "Filii in Filio. Ecriture, Tradition, Théologie," *Nouvelle Revue Théologie* 65 (1938), 551-82, 681-702.

said, "Behold what manner of love the Father has bestowed upon us, that we should be called children of God, and such we are" (1 John 3:1). We are his sons, and we are this because of an almost biological, physical process. God did not simply give us a legal signature, but his own blood, in his Son.

This is the reality we continually try to live up to, the reality of the mystical body. This is Christianity. Christianity means that we are incorporated into a new life with a new heart, the heart of Christ. This is precisely the conception of St. Paul, who uses the formula "in Christo" about one hundred sixty times. St. Paul's expression "in Christ" should discredit in advance any attempt to divide Christianity into dogma, ethics, cult, and so forth. For St. Paul "in Christ" is the reality which is in itself dynamic life and which produces a new heart whose source is Christ. This transformation—through which we go willingly, although we are almost forced to go—is precisely the law of Christ, which is at the center of our morality. If we have the law of Christ, then we need no other law. But if we observe Christianity simply because it is commanded, then we are not guided by the Spirit. The typical feature of the Christian is that he has the spirit of Christ. The Christian has this interior law, which is in itself a new dynamism. Therefore, when we say with St. Paul that the mystery of Christ is to live in Christ, we sum up our entire Christian experience.[15]

Traditional catechetics

If we study catechesis historically, it is remarkable to note that the very first formulas, the Creeds, though apparently trinitarian formulas, do actually center around the mystery of Christ. They *seem* to be trinitarian—we believe in the Father, we believe in the Son, we believe in the Holy Spirit. Recent scholarship, however, has shown that they are essentially Christological and centered around the mystery of salvation.[16] The first part of the Creed, belief in God the Father, is only a preparation for the mystery of Christ. Everything that happened from creation until Christ is simply a wonderful preparation by the Father, who was fitting mankind for sonship in Christ. The second part of the Creed is obviously the mystery of Christ realized. The third part, belief in the Holy Spirit and the Church, is the mystery of Christ prolonged through his Spirit in his Church, his body. Hence the earliest catechetical formulas explain the mystery of Christ.

This type of catechesis continued until the famous *Catechismus Romanus* (1566) of the Council of Trent. This catechism, unfortunately, never became popular because it was overshadowed by the catechetical works of St. Peter Canisius and St. Robert Bellarmine. Their catechisms were translated into every language, while the official *Catechismus Romanus*, written by four Dominicans at the request of the Council of Trent, was practically ignored. Yet the Roman Catechism is actually a beautiful expression of early tradition. Unfortunately, in the later catechisms Christianity becomes complicated. But if religion is complicated, it ceases to be Christianity.[17]

In the early catechetical formulas, as in the formulas of Cyril of Jerusalem or St. Augustine—and even the Roman Catechism—Christianity is simple. It is a beautiful circle of love coming from God to man and returning from man to God, with Christ as its center: first, what God did and does for us in Christ; second, how we are to respond to God in Christ.

Part One includes two sections, the Creed and sacraments. The Creed comprises the first section and explains the wondrous deeds of God (*mirabilia Dei*), what God has

15 B. Häring, *The Law of Christ*. Westminster, Maryland 1961. P. A. Liégé, O.P., *What Is Christian Life?* New York 1961.
16 To the books by F. X. Arnold referred to in Chapter One, note 9, add J. A. Jungmann, *Handing on the Faith, A Manual of Catechetics*. New York, 1959. See also Jungmann, *Glaubensverkündigung im Lichte der Frohbotschaft*. Innsbruck 1963. pp. 21-23.
17 See F. X. Arnold, especially *Dienst am Glauben*. Freiburg 1948. Chapter II.

actually done for us. These deeds are not mere records of history, something wonderful but now past. They are present realities. It is essential that we link the present with the past. Even St. Thomas interpreted one of the last articles of the Creed, "Credo communionem sanctorum," not in the masculine (that is, "I believe in the communion of the saints") but "communionem sanctarum rerum," "I believe in the communion of holy things." This gave him the connecting link with the second section; namely, the sacraments. The sacraments are the clearest way to show that the *mirabilia Dei* are not mere historical deeds, but actually continue in the present. The very same God, in Christ, continues to show today in me, in the Church, that he is a wonderful Father. This is why the sacraments are the second section of this first part in catechesis: what God did and does for us in Christ.

If we explain the Creed as if it were links of a chain, then we run the risk of losing the dynamic togetherness of the mystery. The presentation of God's love for us should be the major concern of our catechesis, because Christianity is primarily concerned with God's loving initiative. Unless we can shout at the end of Part One, with our whole being, "And we have come to know, and have believed, the love that God has in our behalf," as St. John writes in his first Epistle (1 John 4:16), it is useless to begin Part Two, which is our response to the first part. When we begin therefore (as we so often do in catechesis) to mix up the commandments with Part One, everything becomes confused. Unless we are convinced that God loves us, why love him in return? If, on the other hand, the first part is clear, then Part Two follows automatically. Only love is an answer to love; in love man answers the Father in Christ.

Part Two deals with the commandments and prayer, especially the Our Father. Here we should speak more of 'The Commandment' and less of the commandments.[18] Commandments are not the specific characteristic of

Christianity, for we have only one *commandment*, the spirit of love, the spirit of Christ. If we understand this, then the commandments become a way to express our love; they are an opportunity to show our Father that we actually know and love him. If we do not understand 'The Commandment,' we may fulfill the ten commandments materially, but actually not be Christian at all.

This is no mere theory. I know hundreds of Christians who are perfect citizens, but who have not even the first degree of Christianity. They are always in order with themselves, with others, and with God (so they think); but a great chasm exists between God and them because there is no effective communication between the two. The situation is analogous to a person who says someone is his friend, though he never talks with him. This is why commandments and prayer are always connected; prayer is the normal contact between two persons who know each other and desire to meet in a communion of love.

How the dynamic presentation was lost

In the last forty years or so the Church has little by little recovered the dynamic concept of Christianity: the *kerygma* or *evangelization*. Let us pause here, because in many countries Christianity is still being presented as teaching, instruction, information, and the like. The great stress is on doctrine. It is important for us to understand the events that have caused this situation, because some people are still reluctant to accept the kerygmatic approach because they fear it departs from tradition. We must show, therefore, that the type of catechesis most of us learned when we were children was actually an unfortunate deviation from the true tradition of catechesis in the Church.

18 P. A. Liégé, O.P., *What Is Christian Life?* Chapter VI.

Discussing evangelization, Father Liégé stated: "It is a fact that in the Catholic Church little by little primacy has been given to 'doctrinal teaching' and that the stage of kerygma has almost entirely disappeared from catechesis. Doubtless it was thought to be safeguarded when children were baptized in Christian countries and received their education in the faith as from a mother. But what is worse is that the same optimism and the same methods were transplanted to mission countries, where 'evangelization' and the catechumenate were imperative."[19]

This describes the situation as it is in our own day. If we examine most of our mission catechisms, we discover that they are merely "adapted" translations of European catechetical books or catechisms which reflected a heavy doctrinal emphasis.

The polemics of the Counter- Reformation

Two major deviations led to the loss of a dynamic Christianity in Europe. The first was a carryover from the Counter-Reformation. At the time of the Reformation the Church became aware that something must be done to prevent the spread of the reformers' errors. Hence men like Sts. Peter Canisius and Robert Bellarmine wrote catechisms to summarize orthodox Catholic teaching. However, they so arranged their catechisms as to give special, not to say exclusive, consideration to those points that were under the fire of the reformers.

Take, for instance, the approach of Peter Canisius to grace—which, incidentally, still influences many catechisms today. (It is still alive in the present Japanese catechism). Canisius was certainly a great theologian: but he was concerned only with the situation brought about by the reformers. They denied the human element in grace to such an extent that grace became some kind of garment covering the unchanged sinfulness of man. They believed that God acts *as if* we were justified by attributing the merits of Christ to us. Instead of seeing us in our sinfulness, the reformer sees only the merits of Christ, which apply to everyone equally. This conception supposes the elimination of merit and of the distinction between saints. The internal change in man through which he becomes a son of God was misunderstood by Luther.

Canisius clarified the Catholic position on justification by adding a whole new section on this subject instead of a single chapter.[20] And in this entire section the most fundamental notion of grace is omitted, the aspect of *donum increatum*. The new presence of God in man, the indwelling of the Holy Spirit, is not mentioned in this catechism because these ideas were not touched by the reformers. They had attacked only the human element of grace, with the result that the whole emphasis was given to the controversies around actual grace or the *donum creatum* in habitual grace.

This represented a departure from the traditional church teaching, especially as it came from the Greek Fathers. When, for example, the Macedonians in the fourth century denied that the Holy Spirit was God, men like Athanasius,[21] Gregory of Nazianzen,[22] or Cyril of Alexandria[23] answered their objections as follows: "You deny that the Holy Spirit is God. Why? You admit that we are divinized through grace. But if you look for the origin of this divinization, you find it in the Holy Spirit's gift to us. In the fifth and eighth chapters of St. Paul's Epistle to the Romans we read that we are children of God because the Holy Spirit has been given to us. How can he make us children of God if he is not himself God?" Notice that in this controversy the idea of divinization through grace is more central than the idea of the Holy

19 "Evangélisation"; in *Catholicisme* edited by J. Jacquemet. Paris 1954. IV, col. 757.
20 His *Summa Doctrinae Christianae* has 1022 pages dealing with "De Justitia" and only 813 for everything else.
21 See, for instance, PG 26:585G-588A.

22 "If the Holy Spirit is not God, how can He deify us?" PG 36:137B; 252; 165A; 304A.
23 PG 73:137AB. See also B. Fraigneau-Julien, "L'inhabitation de la Trinité dans l'âme selon Saint Cyrille d'Alexandrie," *Revue des Sciences Religieuses* 30 (1956), 136-56.

Spirit's divinity. This dispute gives us an insight into the consciousness of the early Church, especially in its awareness to the divine element in the new creature reborn of grace.[24] After the Reformation this consciousness gradually disappeared.

In St. Robert Bellarmine's treatise on the Church we have an example of this one-sidedness.[25] (Bellarmine was a great theologian, and whenever he is not preoccupied with the reformers his views on the Church are rich and balanced.) Attacking the reformers for denying the visibility of the Church, Bellarmine overemphasized the Church's visible, juridical aspect in his definition of the Church: "The Church is an assembly and congregation of baptized men who, under obedience of the Roman Pontiff, profess the same faith and law of Christ."[26] The main emphasis is on the characteristics that distinguish the true Church from a heretical community. In explaining these characteristics much of the richness of the traditional concept was lost.

For instance, the sanctity of the Church is viewed by Bellarmine not ontologically—as tradition had done until that time—but in an ethical fashion: the Church is holy not as the community of all those who are in grace, but because her members are "holy." The "communion of saints" no longer refers to the spiritual union of members united in grace by the power of the Holy Spirit, but to the fact that "Christians profit by the prayers and good works in the Church, just as all members of the human body profit by whatever good is done by one member."[27]

As for the unity of the Church, Bellarmine sees it as rooted in the hierarchy rather than in the Holy Spirit. It is remarkable to see in his catechism how the link between the Holy Spirit (eighth article of the Creed) and the Church (ninth article) has disappeared—even though previously this unity had always been stressed. It is hardly necessary to point out the unfortunate consequences of these changes.

The first major deviation of catechetics, then, was due to an excessive concern to answer the errors of the reformers. Still greater and more fatal than this deviation was the moralistic and anthropocentric turn that catechetics took at the time of the Enlightenment.[28] Because of its importance we will discuss this point at some length.

The anthropocentric moralism of the Enlightenment

Disillusioned, tired by religious struggles and confessional polemics, the spokesmen of the "scientific century" thought that they could relegate the problems of religious instruction to a secondary plane. Since the struggle over religious issues had divided religion, there was no longer hope of solving problems by religion, but by *reason*, which is common to all men. A book by Immanuel Kant, *Religion within the Limits of Pure Reason* (1793), reflects this spirit.

As a result the preaching of the Church, especially catechesis, was cut off from its intimate relation to God's redeeming work and revelation. It became something to be discussed by men. The message was no longer understood as the creative and revealing word of God continuing in the Church, as the meaning of the term *catechein* suggests. It was the human word rather than the word of God. Religion became a branch of classroom teaching; and the theologically significant word "catechist" was

24 For a balanced view of the historical changes in the message of grace see Josef A. Jungmann, S.J., *The Good News Yesterday and Today*, translated (abridged) and edited by W. Huesman, S.J. New York 1962. pp. 41-55.
25 Jungmann, *Glaubensverkündigung im lichte der Frohbotschaft*, pp. 107-13. See F. X. Arnold, *Grundsatzliches und Geschichtliches zur Theologie der Seelsorge*. Freiburg 1949. pp. 80-83; M. Ramsauer, S.J., "Die Kirche in den Katechismen," *Zeitschrift für Katholische Theologie* 173 (1951), 146 ff.
26 *Christianae doctrinae latior explicatio.* Kempten 1728. p. 57. See Ramsauer, "Die Kirche

in den Katechismen," *Zeitschrift für Katholische Theologie* 173 (1951), 147.
27 *Kleiner Katechismus*, edited by Krawutzky (1873), p. 29; quoted by Arnold, *Grundsatzliches und Geschichtliches zur Theologie der Seelsorge*, p. 82.
28 For what follows see F. X. Arnold, especially *Grundsatzliches und Geschichtliches zur Theologie der Seelsorge*, pp. 69-104; 105-54; J. Rabas, *Katechetisches Erbe der Aufklärung.* Herder 1963.

replaced by "professor" or "teacher of religion," which was considered more refined.

The emphasis now shifted from the divine element in religion and salvation history to the human element. No longer did dogma play the leading role, but morals—man's part. Up to this time the unchanged principle had been first dogma, then morals. Now the order is reversed. Morality, it was said, is the principle object of the Bible; dogma holds a far less important place there. To the question "What dogmas should we teach?" the answer was: Whatever contributes somehow to men's betterment, peace, or the performance of duty. The great dogmas and mysteries of salvation were now viewed as *theoretical aspects* of Christianity, and insufficiently valued.

The catechisms of the sixteenth century—probing for the meaning of Christian existence—began with the question "What is a Christian?" The cathechisms of the Enlightenment began with the philosophical questions: "What is man?" "Why (for what purpose) are we on earth?" The Roman Catechism stressed first what God has done for our salvation; whereas the catechisms of the Enlightenment stressed what *man* must do to save himself.

This catechetical anthropocentrism had dangerous consequences. The unity, order, and depth of the Good News based upon revelation and the economy of salvation were greatly impaired, and the main idea and structure of catechesis were basically changed. It is significant to see that the theological structure and intrinsic connection between the main parts of the catechism, as found in the Roman Catechism, were misunderstood and severely criticized by men like Wessenberg, vicar general of Constance. In particular, the link between the Creed and the sacraments was lost.

This moralistic-anthropocentric point of departure led to a new structure in the catechism: 1) dogma, 2) commandments, and 3) sacraments as a help to keeping the commandments. Thus the place of the sacraments was dislocated. Their connection with the redeeming death and continuing presence of the glorified Lord was obscured and their meaning for Christian life was lost. They became means to virtue and were taught *after* the commandments.

This change continued in neo-scholastic catechisms, such as the famous catechism by Joseph Deharbe, a Jesuit (1847). The Deharbe catechism, however, did mark definite progress, combining theological accuracy with clarity of ideas and definitions. As far as arrangement of content was concerned, however, it continued in error. To make a long story short, the anthropocentric deviation of the Enlightment influenced catechetics until our day.

The effect of the time of the Enlightenment on the sacraments deserves our further study. Presented as something that *we* (by receiving them) must do for our salvation and placed *after* the commandments, the sacraments were no longer seen in proper relation to the redeeming death of Christ and faith in him. They were not considered as memorials of the Passion nor as signs of faith that justify. They were merely means to help man keep the commandments. Far from being seen as transcendent signs and sacramental vehicles of Christ's redemptive death and resurrection, they appear as means to virtue. Thus the true relation between sacraments and morality was blurred and even distorted. In such a catechesis, semi-pelagian conception can easily creep in. One can be misled into believing that our salvation is found more in the action and will of man than in the redeeming work of Christ.

A further difficulty was the separation of the catechesis of the sacraments from that of faith. This separation obscured the relation between the sacraments and our redemption as continuing in and through the presence of the glorified Christ. As a result, practically the only connection between the sacraments and Christ was the thesis on institution and the power of bestowing them, which Christ claims as his own. Faith is no longer seen as an indispensable condition for the efficacy of the sacraments or as the basis on which the whole sacramental world and the sacramental communication of salvation rests. In contrast, tradition has fondly called them *sacramenta fidei*,[29] attributing their power to the *fides passionis*. If, therefore, catechesis disregards the meaning of the sacraments and fails to connect them properly with Christ's death or refer the sacramental grace to that *fides passionis*, then we lose sight of the fundamental meaning of faith in the sacramental act.

It is for this reason that the sixteenth-century catechisms placed faith at the beginning of the baptismal act. We read, for instance, in the catechism of Dietenberger (1530): "Sacramental baptism demands three important things: faith, water, and the divine Word, and none of these may be lacking. Water and the word do not suffice, the word and water are nothing without faith."[30] The Roman Catechism (1566) followed the same line, linking the sacrament with the word of Christ: "He who believes and is baptized will have life everlasting."[31] With reference to infant baptism it states that "when children are baptized they receive the sacrament not on the strength of their own faith, but of the faith of their parents—if they are Christian—and if not, of the faith of the community of saints, as St. Augustine says. For we rightly believe that they are presented for baptism by all those who wish them to be baptized, and whose love guides them into unity with the Holy Spirit."[32]

The same may be said of all the other sacraments. They are based on faith. Hence the Contarini catechism says, referring to St. Thomas: "Sacraments are exterior and sensible signs of the invisible grace which is bestowed through them *on account of faith in Christ's death* by which our sins are forgiven."[33]

If, then, we no longer see the intimate connection between the sacraments and Christ's redeeming death, if the *fides passionis* in the sacramental act is not underlined in catechesis, a great loss ensues. This loss must be considered an unhappy consequence of the separation between catechesis of the sacraments and catechesis of dogma.

There is still more. Not only the structure of the catechism and the relation between dogma and the sacraments were unbalanced as a result of the anthropocentric point of view of the Enlightenment, but even the kerygmatic presentation of the *central mysteries of Christianity* were affected. The incarnation, passion, resurrection, and ascension of the Savior are considered as salvific deeds that are past and completed, rather than as deeds that transcend space and time and reach into our own times. All too often the Christian mysteries are presented in the catechisms under their *historical* aspect and not their *liturgical* aspect, by which they are contained and continued into the present.

This fact, deplored by Hirscher in his fiery polemic on the relationship between the Gospel and scholasticism,[34] is both cause and the consequence of the catechetical separation of the central mysteries; that is, of dogma from the sacraments and grace. Indeed, one cannot separate the explanation of the symbol and the catechesis of grace and the sacraments without depriving both of their religious depth and kerygmatic power. When grace and the sacraments are cut off from their vital source, the redeeming act of God in Christ becomes blurred, the sacramental act ceases to be personal, and grace takes on a profane sense. On the other hand, the isolated presentation of the symbol, without reference to the sacraments and to grace,

29 See, for instance, St. Thomas, *Summa Theologica* III, q. 62, 6.
30 Quoted by Christoph Moufang, *Die katholischen Katechismen des 16 Jahrhunderts*. Mainz 1881. p. 80.
31 *Catechismus Romanus*, II, cap. 2, q. 39.
32 *Ibid.*, cap. 2, q. 33.

33 Moufang, *Die katholischen Katechismen des 16 Jahrhunderts*, p. 542. (Italics added.)
34 Johann Baptist Hirscher, *Über das Verhältnis des Evangeliums zu der theologischen Scholastik der neuesten Zeit im katholischen Deutschland*. Tübingen 1823.

endangers our correct understanding of the *sense and sal-vific meaning* of the redemptive acts of Christ. It reduces them to mere *events*. We lose sight of the wonderful continuity linking Bethlehem, Calvary, and the sacramental, liturgical action of the Church.

This was the second major deviation in catechetics from the traditional method of the Church. It has been treated in detail here because we are still feeling its effects today.

The kerygmatic movement

By the beginning of this century Europe had become, to an alarming degree, a quasi-missionary continent. After World War I, in particular, the increasing awareness of Europe's situation forced theologians and pastors to realize that a different catechetical approach was called for. For centuries the Church—despite the fact that catechesis was wrongly oriented—was able to rely on the home, the general Christian environment, and the school for true Christian formation. Now things were changed. The Church could no longer count on the milieu, because the milieu itself was thoroughly materialistic. She soon realized that something had to be done in catechetics.

Thus the modern catechetical movement began. Starting with Jungmann's *Frohbotschaft* in 1936, it led to the German Catechism, the product of fifteen years' collaboration in the catechetical field. The proponents of the new movement returned to the kerygma; that is, to the core of Christianity, discarding the scholastic and historical accretions that had forced the Christian message into types of human categories and robbed it of its dynamism.

At Eichstätt, Germany, the kerygmatic movement reached its peak, perhaps, when hundreds of catechists from all over the world gathered to study the full meaning of the kerygmatic movement.[35] The best commentary on Eichstätt's contribution to the missionary approach is the summary (made at Bangkok) of the principles developed at Eichstätt to guide the catechetical renewal.[36]

1 *Basic idea:* The catechetical apostolate is a mission imparted by the Church to participate in Christ's proclamation of the good news of salvation. The whole of catechetics is to be inspired and governed by this idea.

2 *Aim:* The aim of the catechetical apostolate is not knowledge as such, but living faith—man's response to God's call (message).

3 *Message:* The emphasis is to be on content more than on method. As for content, we should stress the central theme of God's love accomplished in Jesus Christ (dead, risen, and living in his Church), presented as a gospel (good news) oriented to life.

4 *Method:* Methodology must follow the dynamics of faith: present the religious facts, unfold their religious meaning, and stimulate a personal, vital response to God's call. As such method is a handmaid, but an indispensable one. In all its phases it needs thorough adaptation to those to be catechized.

5 *Fourfold presentation of the faith:* Genuine catechetics requires the sound blending of a fourfold presentation of the faith: through the Bible, liturgy, Church's *magisterium*, and Christian witness. Systematic teaching is not to be begun before the age of ten or twelve, and even then needs to be biblical and liturgical in orientation.

6 *The Catechist:* Because the teacher of religion is Christ's spokesman and witness, he is more important than the textbook. He must personally assimilate the message. He must build up his religious life from the message and harmonize it with his professional training.

7 *Textbooks:* Textbooks are at the service of the teacher and the pupils. Those taking into account the development of present-day theology are a necessity. Outdated texts cannot be modernized by mere modification or revision.

Modern catechetics is basically a spiritual, theological, and pastoral renewal, not just a methodological and psychological advancement.[37]

And yet, notwithstanding the validity and positive concern of these principles for missionary catechetics, the fact

---

35 The Eichstätt Papers (in English, *Teaching All Nations*) were also translated into German, French, and Spanish.

36 See A. M. Nebreda, S.J., *Distinguishing the Different Stages in Missionary Preaching.* Rome 1962. p. 10.

37 "East Asian Study Week on Mission Catechetics (Bangkok)," *Lumen Vitae* XVII (1962), 721.

remained that the kerygmatic renewal had developed and concerned itself primarily with the situation in Christian countries. Its aim was to awaken and stimulate faith. Thus the missionaries left Eichstätt with a sense of uneasiness regarding the applicability of these principles to their own situations. For them faith could not be the point of departure. Their main aim was to set up the conditions for faith. For this reason some missionaries and pastors of quasi-missionary situations frowned on the kerygmatic renewal as not meeting their particular problem. Their task was not to foster the faith of believers but to help the nonbeliever to belief.

Admittedly, the Eichstätt Study Week did not probe this problem. Therefore the meeting at Bangkok in the fall of 1962 addressed itself to the question of preparing non-Christians for faith. For the first time in the modern history of mission catechetics an answer was sought to this basic question.[38]

Distinction between catechetics and kerygma

Before discussing Bangkok I should like to point out the contribution of the French school to the catechetical renewal. The German concern was directed primarily to people who were at least nominally Christian. Faith was the point of departure. For the French, faith was the point of arrival. Their approach was primarily missionary, and hence helpful to the missions.

For several decades French theologians and pastors had been conscious of the growing de-Christianization among their people. It was normal, therefore, that they should consider the missionary question and the kerygma.[39] For the French it was no longer a question of revivifying a languid faith, but one of converting pagans. French pastors preparing children for solemn Communion realized that, unless something were done, these children would return to a home where no one believed. Moreover, the home situation was such that it might even prevent the child from continuing to live his faith. In such a situation the old type catechesis seemed terribly inadequate.

The French realized this. The situation led them to conclude that the first presentation of the message to non-Christians, whether we call it kerygma, evangelization, or missionary preaching, had to be something completely different from catechesis proper.

Father Liégé, a leading authority on this point, wrote: "In what does evangelization consist precisely? The word is not a synonym for *catechesis:* in fact, catechesis in its general sense designates any transmission of the Word of God in the life of the Church. *Evangelization constitutes the first stage of the catechesis leading to conversion,* a distinct and fundamental stage and, considered in itself, previous to any sacramental practice."[40] Evangelization emphasizes the *dynamic aspect* of God's word (God's word judging and challenging, word of power and fruitfulness), whereas catechesis stresses *noetic aspects* (word of truth and wisdom generating contemplative faith).[41]

Father Liégé develops the relation between catechesis and kerygma still further:

> One must avoid opposing the faith of conversion, by which the believer throws in his lot with Jesus Christ, and the faith of knowledge, by which the same believer adheres interiorly to the totality of the Creed. Conversion includes a global acknowledgment of the truth of Jesus Christ, which is to be further developed. The whole catechesis, the whole dogma, is already contained in the Mystery of Christ. For the Catholic Creed is not to be compared to a chain composed of equal links, but rather to the solar spectrum in which all the colors are blended in a luminous synthesis, or to a blossom issuing from a seed. This is why any catechesis presumes the first stage of the encounter with Jesus Christ, which constitutes evangelization.[42]

---

38 *Ibid.,* pp. 720-21.
39 See *Distinguishing the Different Stages in Missionary Preaching,* pp. 10-12. Notes 45-51 list the main representatives of the French school.
40 "Evangélisation"; in *Catholicisme,* IV, col. 756.
41 *Ibid.,* col. 756.
42 *Ibid.,* col. 758.

It is obvious, then, that we suffer from a terminological confusion, and that the word *catechesis* is continually being used in a double sense: a wider sense that refers to "any transmission of the word of God," and a narrower sense that distinguishes it from the kerygma which it develops and explains. In the first sense of the word kerygma is *included* and in the second sense it is *excluded*. The dual usage leads to confusion.

Toward a uniform terminology The contribution of Father Domenico Grasso toward a solution to this problem is significant. In an article published in 1960, Father Grasso proposes the triple distinction of evangelization, catechesis, and homily as the three stages in the transmission of the message.[43] The distinction can be clearly seen in the early Church, where kerygma was preached to pagans, catechesis to catechumens, and homily to the faithful. He believes that the triple distinction is still valid today, both in mission countries and in de-Christianized countries.

Father Grasso also pointed out that kerygma and catechesis had different goals. The purpose of kerygma is to convert. The purpose of catechesis is to initiate the new believer into the mystery of Christ and to assist him to develop a Christian personality. It seems to me that we may add a further distinction: in catechesis, faith in Christ is the point of departure; in kerygma, faith is the point of arrival.[44]

A quotation from Father Henry's preface to the French edition of the Eichstätt Papers sums up the need for a clear distinction between kerygma and catechesis:

> Catechesis aims at the converted, at people who have already received, accepted, understood kerygma . . . It is therefore really dangerous and often unfortunate to present catechesis . . . to those who have not received kerygma, or to permit entrance into the catechumenate, and *a fortiori* into the Church of the baptized, of these people . . . Without kerygma, catechesis runs the risk of being no more than mere religious teaching which does not really

penetrate into the heart of the believer, since there is no point of entry to a faith which is as yet non-existent. With kerygma, on the contrary, catechesis acquires its true standing.[45]

The Bangkok Study Week on mission catechetics

In an effort to advance the line of Eichstätt, the Bangkok meeting directed attention primarily to the missionary aspect of catechetics. It brought into fuller focus the different stages of missionary preaching, and stressed the importance of the decisive stage: evangelization, or kerygma. Having conversion as its aim, this stage is at the heart of missionary preaching. Nothing can take its place.

Let us repeat here the main features of evangelization as described at Bangkok. The official statement reads:

> Once the believer has acquired a sense of God and appears spiritually ready to accept God's Message, a short resumé of salvation history is to be presented in such a way that the compelling fact of Christ as the Lord appears with striking clarity. In a technical world where man feels himself lost "in a lonely crowd," stressing such facts as God coming to us in Christ, Christ living among us as our friend and personally loving each of us, helps to awaken man to hope, and helps to evoke conversion.[46]

As is evident even from this short summary, the Study Week carefully stressed the key elements of the message: salvation history, centering on the Person of Christ and insisting on the fact of Christ as Lord. Finally, the Study Week emphasized the fact of Christ's continuing action in men's lives today—a modern statement of the famous *appetibilitas* which St. Augustine developed so well in his catechetical instruction.[47]

---

43 Domenico Grasso, S.J., "Il kerigma e la predicazione," *Gregorianum* 41 (1960), 424-50.
44 For a fuller treatment see A. M. Nebreda, S.J., *Distinguishing the Different Stages in Missionary Preaching*, pp. 12-14.
45 *Renouvellement de la catéchèse*, pp. 17-18.
46 "East Asian Study Week on Mission Catechetics," *Lumen Vitae* XVII (1962), 725.

47 His classic *De Catechizandis rudibus* deals with this stage of evangelization, rather than with catechesis proper, as has all too often been taken for granted. See D. Grasso, "Saint Augustine évangélizateur," *Parole et Mission* 6 (1963), 357-78.

The point that was perhaps most strongly stressed at Bangkok was *conversion*, the aim and fruit of evangelization or kerygma. The Bangkok report says: "Shock is the internal spiritual change in a man whereby he accepts Christ as the Lord. The catechist, by close observation, can recognize this conversion by such signs as repentance, prayer, a new eagerness to meet Christ, living according to the Christian pattern, and so forth."[48]

The Bangkok report stressed the importance of conversion as the boundary between the precatechumenate and the catechumenate:

> Although very important, the question of when the catechesis proper is to begin should be determined by the factor of conversion, which clearly separates the precatechumenate from the catechumenate . . . Without this conversion the catechist would be defending and proving, thus making the catechumenate mere intellectual instruction and destroying its essential character, which is to build religious knowledge based on faith. It should, therefore, be the careful concern of the catechist to detect the signs of conversion.[49]

I have discussed elsewhere and at length the problem of conversion as a keystone of the whole missionary approach, so I need not go into detail here.[50]

48 "East Asian Study Week on Mission Catechetics," *Lumen Vitae* XVII (1962), 725.
49 *Ibid.*, p. 726. See also A. Turck, "Aux origines du catéchuménat," *Revue des sciences philosophiques et théologiques* 48 (1964), 20-31, especially pp. 28, 29 T. Maertens, *Histoire et*

Pastorale du catéchuménat et du baptême. Bruges 1962.
50 See "Conversion: Key-stone of the Missionary Process," *Lumen Vitae* XVIII (1963), 661-78.

Kerygma
in
crisis?

A major pastoral advance within the Church has been the recovery of the dynamic aspect of the Christian message.[1] Yet in spite of advances such as this, there are situations that still give us pause and invite our serious reflection. Take the following incident that happened in Japan.

At a national catechetical meeting in 1956, it was decided that, since writing a new catechism was too difficult a task at the moment, the existing catechism should be revised. It was thought that Japan was not yet ready to prepare an altogether new catechism.

In 1959, three years later, after extensive consultation with Japanese priests, it was decided that a Japanese catechism ought to have an "apologetic" orientation.[2] The

---

1 See the beautiful article of Bishop Emmett Carter, "Head and Heart," *America* 109 (1963), 40-43, where he compares the meaning and aim of the kerygmatic renewal with those of Vatican Council II and the spirit of *aggiornamento* brought into the Church by John XXIII.

2 See P. Pfister, "Revision of the Catechism. Its Development and Aim," *Japan Missionary Bulletin* 13 (1959), 476.

wording of the decision reflected an insufficiently nuanced conception of transmitting the Christian message.[3] Confusion deriving from terminology is still widespread and needs to be cleared up, as the Bangkok conference urged.[4] Catechesis is one thing; apologetics is another. Elsewhere I have shown that catechesis proper, if it deserves the name, presupposes and insists on faith as its point of departure.[5] It has as its aim a deeper understanding, *fides quaerens intellectum*—faith trying to understand. Apologetics, however, leans heavily on proofs, or at least on things that are viable and clear to a reasonable man.

Prescinding from terminology, the decision of the Japanese regarding the need for an apologetic catechism gives us food for thought. It shows that they were aware, as are most pastors, that a purely catechetical approach is often impossible. If you start by presuming that your audience believes, you are frequently just begging the question. This was the case in Japan. The Japanese missionaries felt a need to prepare the people before introducing them to the kerygma. The kerygma is a challenge from God urging man to make a decision. But before man can respond, he must realize he has been addressed. And that is the problem. If you start by presenting the Christian fact, you sense somehow that the audience feels as if you were talking to somebody else. They remain untouched. The words they hear mean little or nothing to them. They do not feel themselves challenged.

Let us put the discussion in the form of a question. "Is a crisis developing in the kerygmatic movement?"

A purely kerygmatic approach

Thought evolves in a sort of dialectical movement. Catechetics, after a few centuries of one-sided insistence upon the doctrinal aspect of the message, is now deeply concerned about the dynamic aspect of the kerygma. The pendulum has changed course and is now swinging in the opposite direction. Is there a danger in all this? Is a purely kerygmatic approach the answer? This is the point I would now like to explore.

It is significant that even Protestants are questioning the purely kerygmatic approach they had been stressing for more than a century. Take, for example, the famous Dutch missionary theologian Kraemer. In his earlier works he took a pessimistic stance, holding that when a culture is not Christian it is hostile to God. In recent years he and other Protestant theologians are showing signs of a change of position.[6] It appears that missionary experience has shown them that something must be wrong. It is easy to say that all should become Christians. It is still easier to say that once they have heard the message, it is their responsibility. But when you face the same unsuccessful mission experience for one hundred years, as in Japan, you start wondering.

In Japan the whole Protestant mission approach has been thoroughly kerygmatic. Now disciples of a man like Karl Barth begin asking themselves earnestly whether this is the correct approach. Barth is an extreme example of a kerymatic theologian. He denies even the possibility of a natural theology, vigorously stressing that there is no way for man to meet God except to kneel down and accept faith as a gift. Now former students of Barth are beginning to question his stand. In 1959 one of them wrote an astonishing article in Japanese called "Kerygma or Apologetics?" "I believe," was his conclusion, "that for Japan neither the Barthian formula—kerygma, not apologetics—nor the alternative that is often presented in Europe—either apologetics or kerygma—is valid. We

3 I have explained my views at length in the essay *Distinguishing the Different Stages in Missionary Preaching*. Rome 1962.
4 "East Asian Study Week on Mission Catechetics," *Lumen Vitae* XVII (1962), 717-30.
5 See A. M. Nebreda, S.J., "Conversion: Keystone of the Missionary Process," *Lumen Vitae* XVIII (1963), 661-78.

6 Although still very reserved toward non-Christian cultural values, Hendrick Kraemer has shifted his position somewhat nearer the Catholic attitude with regard to his former works. See his more recent book, *World Cultures and World Religions*. London 1960. Much closer to our position is R. Hammer, *Japan's Religious Ferment*. New York 1962.

need a combination of both, *apologetics for the sake of kerygma.*"[7] I think that, when sufficiently understood, this has been the traditional position of Catholicism. Thus Protestant theologians, it seems, are coming back to what has always been the traditional approach of the Church.

When I left Japan after eight or nine years there, I was shocked to find that there was so much talk against apologetics in Paris, Brussels, and several other places in Europe. People wanted only kerygma. "You must preach the message!" was the battlecry. So I listened and listened and said every time, "I am sorry, I cannot accept this in the light of the Japanese situation." I waited some eight months before I asked to see several of the most outstanding professors in Paris, especially Father Liégé. I had occasion to discuss the matter with most of them, one after the other. I spoke, for instance, with one of the leading pastoral theologians for a whole morning, and he understood my point and said, "Of course, when I condemn 'apologetics,' I mean poor apologetics." Nevertheless, too often the impression is given, I am afraid, that *all* apologetics is today considered not only outdated in some of its concrete realizations but even a bit absurd.

My most interesting experience was with another young professor in Paris. When I explained to him the problem in Japan and the way we tried to solve it, he said: "Father, this is not only a problem for Japan, it is the same here. Look, Father, I must honestly say that we have gone too far in France. . . . If I tell you that more than 90 per cent of the questions I get from my students in technical schools is to be met at the apologetic level, I do not exaggerate. Now what is the use of answering an apologetically loaded question by saying, 'Wait a minute, I am going to tell you what our faith is.' That is absurd. He is asking you, 'How can you explain this?' And you say, 'I do not want to discuss that, now I am going to proclaim what the mystery of Christ is.' After a while the youngster, unimpressed, goes away."

A few weeks later I traveled through several European countries. I visited several catechetical centers and was amused to see that whenever I talked of Japan and our catechetical methods, the people would laugh at me, in a very polite way. But they would laugh. "Father, how strange! This approach is already fifty years old. Today we approach people with the Bible."

I listened patiently and then I asked them very simply, "Where did you study?"

"In Paris, of course."

"Who were your professors?"

"Oh Father . . ., Father . . ., and Father . . ."

"Oh, is that so? I am sorry to tell you that I have just had a very long discussion with all of them and they don't seem to feel as you feel."

All over Europe I have heard former students from Paris and elsewhere say that they need more help. I am convinced that everywhere, not only in missiology and catechesis but also in the whole pastoral field of the Church, we must restudy our whole approach to preparing people for the kerygmatic message. In this task of preparing for the kerygma, apologetics has an important role.[8] In fact it is essential to the kerygmatic approach. When the kerygma is left to the instinctive or to the emotional, it has no roots.[9] What is the good of a seed without knowledge of soil?

Christian faith is indeed a mystery—a mystery of God (grace) and a mystery of man (liberty). But let us not

7 Kano Yamamoto, "Ajia ni okeru senkyoo to gokyoo (Kerygma and Apologetics in Asia)"; in H. R. Fox and K. Yamamoto, *Ajia ni okeru Kirisutokyoo (Christianity in Asia)*. Tokyo 1951. pp. 31-74.

8 In this sense the catechetical study week held at Bangkok in November of 1962 will go down both in the history of missiology and of catechetics as an epoch-making event. For the official papers of the Conference see "East Asian Study Week on Mission Catechetics," *Lumen Vitae* XVII (1962), 717-30.

9 Albert Corvaisier, M.E.P., stresses this point very forcefully. See "Evangélisation et Caté-chèse," *Epiphanie* 2 (1962), 433-40. See also A. M. Henry, O.P., "Le Kérygme dans le ministère de la Parole"; in *L'annonce de l'évangile aujourd'hui*, edited by A. M. Henry. Paris 1962. pp. 107-10.

forget that the faith is also *reasonable*. These are the three qualities which traditional theology has always stressed.

It is right here that the greatest hope of Christianity lies today, provided we know how to make use of it. We must first of all meet people where they are. At this point I always explain to my students Newman's distinction between "reasonable" and "rational." Many people use them interchangeably; and if you consult a dictionary, you will find no distinction. But I believe there is a definite and important distinction behind these words. It is one thing to be "rational" or rationalistic—to be bound up with a one-sided intellectual approach to things; it is another to be "reasonable." Through reason you demonstrate that there are times when it would be unreasonable to be rationalistic. If you try to explain love, for instance, in terms of a "rational" approach, you are embarking on the impossible. A young lady can tell you that. You cannot explain love in terms of the pure reason of Kant. This approach is completely inadequate. Nor can you apply pure reason to the realm of personal values.[10] You will fail because value goes much deeper, too human to be dissected and analyzed by pure reason. The tool is inadequate.[11]

Dechristianized and Marxist infiltrated areas

Pastoral experience confirms what we have just been saying. In the same France where the kerygmatic movement has done wonders, most of the experienced pastors still insist strongly on some kind of apologetics. Take the Dominican, Father Loew, himself a convert and a priest-worker for many years. Father Loew is director of the excellent magazine *Fêtes et Saisons*. In his books, such as his diary of eighteen years of a working mission in Lyons, he notes most clearly that there are cases where you cannot begin with a purely kerygmatic approach.[12] You must first prepare the people for the kerygma. He recalls a small boy shouting "Tarzan, Tarzan" during an explanation of the biblical story of Adam.

The same tendency may be noted in the works of Father Thivollier, who is famous both as a popular missionary in France and as author of several catechetical books for the average man.[13] He is thoroughly apologetic, communicating in a way contemporaries understand. So is Father Feligonde, the Benedictine who is the author of a catechism in two volumes.[14] He explains from the beginning why he must start like this. Whenever you are going to meet an unbeliever, you must begin by approaching him where and as you find him. Another example is a book edited by Girault, devoted largely to stories of converts.[15] There is a story of a man who went from Schopenhauer to Christ. He says, "When I read Pascal, whom I admire, I always wonder if this approach would work with a true atheist?"[16] For a majority of the so-called atheists are really not confirmed in their views. They are more or less wavering. When, however, you meet a true atheist you know it. There is no entry. You have to give him a sort of shock which suddenly opens a crack through which the message can begin to shine.[17]

The same holds true for Germany, where the whole approach in recent years has been thoroughly kerygmatic. Whenever the Church addresses the East German people,

10 How accurate and modern is the diagnosis of Jean Lacroix: "Dans une large mésure, la pensée moderne a reduit la raison à la raison scientifique, et la raison scientifique à un type de science." See "Ce qui chez nous menace la personne humaine"; in *Semaines Sociales*. Clermont 1937. p. 100.

11 It is most enlightening to insist on the different levels of reality and the corresponding levels of human knowledge, as A. Brunner, S.J., and others have repeatedly stressed. See A. Brunner, *Glaube und Erkenntnis*. Munich 1951. A good summary can also be found in the first and second chapters of his treatise on ontology, *Der Stufenbau der Welt*. Munich 1950. The main lines of Brunner's realistic phenomenology can be studied in *La Personne Incarnée*. Paris 1947. For a summary of his ideas see G. McCool, "The Primacy of Intuition," *Thought* 37 (1962), 61-64.

12 J. Loew, O.P., *Journal d'une mission ouvrière*, 1941-1959. Paris 1959. See also *Si vous saviez le don de Dieu*. Paris 1958 and "Les incroyants d'aujourd'hui," *Parole et Mission* 4 (1961), 440-49.

13 A. Thivollier, *Toi qui cherches, toi qui doutes*. Paris 1951. See also the collection *Franc-parler sur la religion*.

14 G. de Feligonde, O.S.B., *L'Armure du chrétien*. Paris 1957.

15 R. Girault, editor, *J'ai rencontré le Dieu vivant*. Paris 1952. See especially "Suggestions pour une théologie missionaire."

16 "De Schopenhauer à Descartes et à Dieu"; in *J'ai rencontré le Dieu vivant*. p. 233.

17 *Ibid.*, p. 223.

who are in close touch with Marxist ideas, it takes an apologetic approach. At the 1958 Katholikentag in Berlin the booklet given to all the participants, *Unsere Sorge der Mensch, Unser Heil der Herr*—was thoroughly apologetic.[18] The authors, a group of eminent theologians and philosophers, were trying to come to grips with the questions people ask there. The same goes for the books of Father Vries and others.[19]

These are the people who are daily facing the true difficulties. Reality forces them to nuance the kerygmatic approach and to prepare the people for it by a kind of threshold apologetics. Let us be perfectly clear. I am not saying that the kerygmatic approach is bad. Nor am I even implying that we should return to the old approach. That would be absurd. I am simply saying that we need to keep a proper balance, "apologetics for the sake of kerygma." This is precisely what I call "pre-evangelization"; namely, preparing men so that the kerygma may have meaning in this milieu or for that individual.

Importance of a prekerygmatic approach in view of the contemporary mentality

Lest there be a misunderstanding here, let me say that we should not view things exclusively in terms of opposition, contradiction, or negation. We should look at them as being complementary. I have spoken of de-christianized areas in France or Marxist-influenced areas in Germany, but what was said applies to the entire world.

Our children, without our realizing it, are growing up with a thoroughly positivistic mentality. (Let us be clear here. Positivism as a *method* is perfectly justified; positivism as a *mentality* is dangerous.) The result is that even in their spiritual life they tend to be positivistic. We must take this into account in our catechetical work with them.

We priests who have studied scientific or scholastic theology must keep in mind that we have been formed in a thoroughly *deductive* mentality. We are familiar with it and its processes. We have no difficulty going from premises to conclusions. We even go through a series of *ergos* with ease. This is not the case with everyone. When I was in Japan I was astonished to see that intelligent people could not follow our deductive way of reasoning. You say, "This is this, therefore." And the poor physicist in front of you, who may be a professor at the university, stares at you blindly. "What do you mean?" he says.

The point I wish to make is that these people have been educated in an *inductive* way, which differs from our method. This gives rise to many difficulties. We do not understand each other.

It would be absurd, almost a blasphemy, for a missionary to try to force people to become deductive thinkers in order to believe. It is our task as apostles to try to apply to *ourselves* the dynamic of faith—to go out of ourselves and to try to appreciate the position of our hearers—to see through their eyes and feel through their hearts.[20] This is not an easy task.

How often in a classroom have we not become exasperated by a boy who interrupts us with a question that seems completely off the point. Yet, if we show our exasperation and ignore his question, we run the risk of appearing to be insincere. For we have repeatedly told him that we are interested in his problems. We must begin to realize that he does not always think according to our neat categories.

I mention this because it is essentially connected with what I consider most important in apologetics. I refer to the whole attitude of speaker and listener. If our hearers suspect us of being insincere for having made a statement and then refusing to defend it when we are legitimately

18 *Unsere Sorge der Mensch—Unser Heil der Herr*, edited by W. Adolph, E. Klausener, and H. Muschalek. Berlin 1958.
19 See, for instance, Joseph de Vries, S.J., *Warum Religion? Die natürlichen Grundlagen des Gottesglaubens*. Berlin 1958. There is a short bibliography on pages 100-07.
20 I consider particularly suggestive the book by Jean Levie, S.J., *Sous les yeux de l'incroyant*. Brussels 1946.

challenged, how can we demand sincerity in a dialogue of them? Sincerity and an openness of mind are essential ingredients of any dialogue between people. Unless these ingredients are present, it is useless to discuss with another any serious issue. You need at least a minimal sincerity and openness. This will thus be the first task of apologetics, to create this climate of sincerity and openness. The minds of many pagans and nonpagans today are subconsciously closed to religion. It is useless to try to discuss it without first preparing the way. We must find common ground and begin our dialogue there. This might be anything.

For example, we can say to them what I sometimes say to my students, "Can you give me reasons why I should not believe?" I try to put myself at their level. I am perfectly honest. If I were not convinced that Christ is Christ, it would be absurd to believe; as St. Paul has said: "We are the most foolish and the most unhappy men on earth." So please show me why I should not believe. This procedure demands a constant effort to purify oneself, to understand the other through his mentality, which is radically different from our own. One never concludes such a dialogue without enriching one's own faith.

Apologetics under fire

Let us now take a close look at the two sides of apologetics. Apologetics has been under fire for years—often with good reason. What are the objections against classical apologetics—the approach we studied and the one in most textbooks today? In 1958 appeared the first volume of a posthumous work of Johann Steffes, formerly professor at Münster. The book purports to be a new apologetics, in which Steffes studies the problem from every angle— from anthropology, sociology, the history of religion, comparative religion, and so forth. It is a monumental work. In twenty-five pages of his introduction he explains why he does not call it apologetics. He calls it *Glaubensbegründung*, which means "foundation of faith," trying to establish our faith. Then in the subtitle he adds, *Christlicher Gottesglaube in Grundlegung und Abwehr*, "Christian faith in fundamental presentation and in defense."[21] He avoids the term apologetics. In the introduction, before devoting more than one hundred pages to the history of apologetics in the Church,[22] he explains why he does not want to use the term.[23]

According to Steffes the two major objections made against apologetics are: (1) "an exaggerated regard for formal abstract reason"; and (2) "a neglect of the revolutions of all kinds in almost every field of knowledge."

The first objection: exaggerated regard

We should have regard for abstract reason. But the problem is that we have too much regard.[24] This gives the impression that we wish to rationalize religion, making of it a kind of idealistic absolute philosophy. We give the impression of presenting divine revelation as if it were a kind of sacred metaphysics. So many textbooks present *De Deo uno* as if God himself had given us no direct idea of what he is like, or better who he is. We present the topic in a philosophical manner, giving the impression the course is merely a continuation of natural theology.

Apologetics is suspected therefore of claiming to prove Christianity to anyone, regardless of his personal position and beliefs. Moreover, it does it on the basis of autonomous reason, a heritage from the Age of Enlightenment, so that the absence of consent can only be imputed to ill will. This was, I fear, my mentality when I first came to Japan. How did I imagine the unbeliever? Either—or; bad brains or bad heart. This may seem like a caricature, but is it? How many apologists present things in such a way as to

21 J. F. Steffes, *Glaubensbegründung. Christlicher Gottesglaube in Grundlegung und Abwehr.* Vol. I. Mainz 1958.

22 *Ibid.*, I, 3-110.
23 *Ibid.*, I, xiii-xvi.
24 *Ibid.*, I, xiii-xiv.

imply, "If you were open, you would see at once." They do not seem to realize that things are far more complicated than that. They fail to take into consideration that we are dealing with a twofold mystery here. We never know where, and how, and how deeply these two mysteries meet. We refer here to those two "abysses" of which Pascal wrote: the mystery of God in man—grace—and the mystery of man in God—freedom. Nor do we know how prepared our hearer is. Will it take years before he is able even to understand the point we are trying to make? Who knows whether the grace of God is calling, at this moment, for a decision in faith? There are many question marks. These, at least, make the apologist a man of respect for God. After all, when we deal with a mystery, everything comes from God.

How dare we conclude, then, that a man's failure to respond is due to his ill will, or some defect of mind? No. When you meet, as I have, thousands of people who do not seem to fall into either of these categories—who are neither idiots nor bad men—you receive a shock. You learn an important lesson which sets you thinking. The problem of faith is a most difficult one. If we are to help the unbeliever, the first thing we must do is to meditate on the tremendous difficulty of reducing to simple lines what is of itself most complex.

I think we can learn a lot from phenomenologists like Husserl, Max Scheler, and others.[25] They teach us a great lesson: truth is one thing; the way man comes to truth is another. We sometimes assume that we are somehow like vessels, more or less uniform. Therefore we conclude, naturally speaking, that if the vessel is sufficiently open and truth is sufficiently there, it must fill the vessel. But things are not quite so simple.

The weight of prejudice

Do any of us realize how thoroughly prejudiced we are? The impact of prejudice on the process of faith has been well described by Newman.[26] In any language "prejudice" is loaded with a negative meaning; we are biased, we are one-sided in our position. I fear we are not sufficiently aware that prejudice is not something we have. We do not *have* prejudice; we *are* prejudiced. If we *had* prejudice, we could easily get rid of it. We could drop it. But you cannot drop yourself into a river. It is clear to any psychologist that prejudice permeates one's whole being. Everything a man has read, seen, heard, thought about, reacted to, his whole life, figures into his prejudice. He can scarcely get rid of that. The only thing to do with a man is to make him conscious of the type and depth of prejudice that is his.

Here we might recall the old scholastic saying, "Quidquid recipitur, ad modum recipientis recipitur." (Whatever is received, is received according to the pattern of the person who receives.) In dealing with our young people or with nonbelievers, it is good to keep in mind that our whole reaction varies according to the degree of personal impact that a certain truth makes upon us. If it is a question of a mathematical truth, of course, this does not touch our life. I have never lost two minutes of sleep over a mathematical truth. Some mathematician might lose his sleep, but that would be on account of his involvement in mathematics as such. A mathematical truth is something that is detached from a man; it is a most depersonalized, not to say impersonal, subject. At this level we can reason with each other quite well.

As soon as the subject begins to touch man at the human level, however, things begin to blur. Politics is a good example. I am reminded here of the words of Dr. Gregorio Marañón, who is a great Spanish thinker, an authority

25 See the interesting book by Raymond Vancourt, *La phénoménologie et la foi*. Tournai 1953.
26 See P. Flanagan, *Newman, Faith and the Believer*. London 1946. J. Artz, *Glaubensbegründung aus dem Persönlichen*. Freiburg 1958.

on endocrinology and a historian with a special interest in the psychological side of historical figures: "In politics the only psychological mechanism which operates a change is conversion, never conviction; and one must always suspect the man who changes when he says that he has been convinced."[27]

I like this quotation because it prepares the way for a clear understanding of what happens when man is touched at his deepest level, that of religion. You just do not *convince* anyone, even at the political level. If the man is really a politician, you will not convince him. It is not a question to be decided by argument. Nor is it a question to be settled with scientific evidence. There are so many thousands of small factors involved that unless the man goes through a kind of conversion, nothing will help. No wonder, then, that at the level of religion sheer argument is of no avail. We must take a man with all his prejudices and try to enter into this sphere of his, remembering always that the initiative is not ours.

It is God who takes the initiative. We know that this man is receiving divine grace which enlightens and calls him. Our job is to cooperate with grace. Here we must constantly remind ourself that God's pedagogy does not follow a schedule. God is always gentlemanlike. He never enters a room unless someone says, "Yes, come in please." This is the picture given us in the third chapter of the Apocalypse: "I stand at the door and knock. If anyone listens to my voice and opens the door to me, I will come in" (Apocalypse 3:20).

When we approach nonbelievers with our categories, forgetting that each is different on account of individual prejudices, we make a serious mistake. We often think that they do not want to believe. No! Very often they cannot. We must at least consider this possibility. It is real. Who knows that this man has received just the type of grace which should convert him today? No one. This is precisely the mystery.

By entering at his level, we shall approach the nonbeliever in a completely different manner—unhurried, unoppressive, and calm. I have been told by the Japanese that what they resent most is the impression given that we want to force something on them. In a sense they are instinctively closer to God's mentality than we. They realize that things in the realm of the spirit defy force and remain wrapped in an atmosphere of mystery.

The second objection The second objection, according to Steffes, is "a neglect of the revolutions of all kinds which have taken place in almost every field of knowledge; in natural science, history of religion, prehistory, sociology, anthropology, psychology, epistemology. Apologetics can be compared to a lawyer who, instead of being objective, wishes only to save his client by any and all means. One doubts the good faith of the apologist who pretends to know everything and who thinks that by multiplying distinctions he can dominate the situation and refute his opponents."[28]

This statement is strong but it is true. I am reminded of a Japanese doctor who served several religious communities in Tokyo. He was not a Catholic, but he had been born in Nagasaki where the Catholic atmosphere is strong and powerful. We became good friends. One day he said to me, "I like you personally, but there is something I hate among you, especially you priests. It is that you seem to know everything."

This should be an important warning for us. We do know God, and in God we have an enlightened vision of things, of the world, of life, of death. But this is quite a different area of knowledge, apart from that scientific

27 "En politique, l'unique mécanisme psychologique du changement est la conversion, jamais la conviction; et l'on doit toujours suspecter celui qui change, quand il dit qu'on l'a convaincu." See

Gregorio Marañón, *Libéralisme et Communisme.* Paris 1961. p. 59.
28 Steffes, *Glaubensbegründung*, I, xiv.

knowledge which every man of science painfully strives after. Let us not present things in a way which leaves the impression that everything is evident. Everything is not evident. Such self-assured dogmatism in a sermon, or in a conversation, or in a classroom can ruin the whole effect of hundreds of other things. We must learn to respect the man of science. Very often he has a sort of embryonic revelation of God, although it often appears in a negative light. If he denies religion or things in religion, he does so, perhaps, because he has a higher idea of religion than what he sees in us. This is one of the lessons of atheism.[29] What many so-called atheists deny is a caricature. Their denial shows us negatively that they do have a certain insight into what God should be like, what religion should be like. It could be a tragedy to destroy their implicit yearning for something higher, something more delicate, something more mysterious.

That is why I always return to the same point. The decisive question in the classroom is not so much the explanation but the whole attitude with which it is given. And the attitude can be detected often by some short comment or even the way we respond to a boy who comes up to ask a question. The expression of interest, the encouraging glance, is already a kind of exchange.

To sum up, therefore, the defects of apologetics in this area are quite obvious. Usually we are accused of conducting a sort of negative apologetics; namely, approaching a person as an enemy, trying to defend, to defend, to defend. The impression given is that apologetics is a question of polemics. But too often from the fire of polemics comes only heat and no light.

Toward a correct appreciation of apologetics The one-sided intellectual approach is one reason why apologetics is out of favor today. We must begin to be more human about it. Father Ramsauer, professor of theology and member of the East Asian Pastoral Institute, gave some enlightening insights on approaching nonbelievers.[30] But as far as apologetics is concerned, he takes what I consider to be a rather typical approach among Catholic theologians. He says that apologetics, being essentially the defense of faith for those who believe, does not need to insist on the elements that might influence the heart and help the conversion process, which is presupposed when we deal with believers. Its only concern is to equip believers intellectually to meet the challenge from the nonbeliever.

When I was in Manila in the fall of 1962, I had a long discussion with Father Ramsauer. He saw my point of view. If you put the question in those terms, of course the positive meaning of apologetics is eliminated a priori.[31] For if apologetics has a meaning for us who believe, but no true meaning for one who does not believe, then we are prolonging the grounds of the nonbelievers' accusation that we are not sincere. For me apologetics must be something that convinces me in such a way that I can express it in a fashion which is valid for the nonbeliever also.[32] I do not mean to oblige anyone to believe. That is not the aim of apologetics. The only one who makes man believe is God.

29 See the following books and articles: J. Maritain, *La signification de l'athéisme contemporain* (Paris 1949); M. I. Congar, "Qui visibiliter Deum cognoscimus," *Maison-Dieu* 59 (1951), 132-61; J. Y. Jolif, "Signification humaine de l'athéisme contemporain," *Economie et Humanisme* 15 (1956), 185-206; J. Lacroix, *Le sens de l'athéisme moderne* (Paris 1959); E. Borne, *Dieu n'est pas mort* (Paris 1961); P. A. Liégé, *What Is Christian Life?* (New York 1961), Chapter IV.

30 M. Ramsauer, S.J., "The Catechetical Task of Disposing the Pagans for the Faith," *Lumen Vitae* XVI (1961), 591-606.

31 The statement of A. McIntyre represents an extreme formulation of this trend: "Belief cannot argue with unbelief; it can only preach to it. . . . The only apology of religion is to describe its content in detail, and then either man will find himself brought to say 'My Lord and my God' or he will not." See *Metaphysical Beliefs*. London 1957. p. 209.

32 This means that if apologetics is to be 'integral,' it must combine the *objective* element— that is, the intellectual proofs explaining the credibility of our faith—and the *subjective* aspect —man as a person in the world to whom we are to speak in his concrete situation. See N. Dunas, "Les problèmes et le statut de l'apologétique," *Revue des Sciences Philosophiques et Théologiques* 43 (1959), 643-80. The author has presented the same ideas in the essay "Pour une proposition kérygmatique de l'évangile aujourd'hui"; in *L'annonce de l'évangile aujourd'hui*, edited by A. M. Henry. pp. 233-314, and particularly pp. 307-09.

We are speaking about conditioning man for faith. I can reverse the proposition and say that there are perhaps thousands of men who have lost their faith or have never arrived at faith because there was no sound apologetic preparation. We are not here speaking of causes. The only real explanation of this complex phenomena of conversion and faith is God's grace, because faith is a gift of God's grace. Yet at the same time and at the same level, as St. Bernard explained, man's liberty is also a cause. These are the two causes. Both are equally responsible as far as causality is concerned. But there is a third line we must keep in mind: the line of the external presentation of the message, which God has decided to use. He could have done everything by himself, without mediation; but he chose to approach man through human instrumentality. Unless this line is free of obstacles, there is no way for God's message to pass to man and shine out so that he can grasp it.[33]

Together with the type of apologetics fit for those who already believe, therefore, we must study the meaning and role of an apologetics for the nonbeliever, before he has faith, as the Bangkok conference pointed out.[34] It should prepare the ground for a man to see the kerygma as a challenge. It should bridge the gap for a dialogue in which you speak the same language with him, not where you talk and talk and he hears but does not feel touched. That is why we must make a clear distinction between bad apologetics and good apologetics. We must not identify apologetics with bad apologetics, as is too often the case. This has been the whole effort of the Church from the very beginning, from men like Justin and Tertullian, down to this very day.[35] Such has been the effort of a layman like Jean Guitton in France, whose life has been dedicated to making it possible for the modern unbeliever to understand what we mean when we say, "Christ is the Lord."[36]

You have all sort of lines. There are lines that *ascend*, as in the case of Jean Guitton. He feels it is better for the modern mind to start with Christ and through Christ arrive at an understanding of Christianity.[37] This is the traditional way. There is also the regressive or *descending* way enunciated by Cardinal Deschamps at the time of the First Vatican Council.[38] When you know church history, you understand many things. St. Augustine explained the two methods in a remarkable fashion. "The apostles saw Christ and had to believe in the Church. We see the Church, but have to believe in Christ." There you have the two types of apologetics. Which is better? I do not know. We must evaluate the particular mentality in each given case; there are different approaches. But certainly, whether we follow the distinction between factual evangelization and verbal evangelization, the fact remains that Christ is best seen today in a community or in an individual. Through this kind of witness the nonbeliever becomes aware of Christ. From this vision of Christ in the Church or the individual, he goes on to discover God wonderfully proclaiming himself, as Father, in Christ.[39]

Another example for our study is Blondel. His whole life was dedicated to showing how human nature is crying out in every cell for God. Every activity, as being, as wishing, as dynamism, is waiting for the call of Christian revelation. How can this be true and yet respect the

33 This is how Father Congar conceives apologetics as the "defensive et justificative fonction" of theology "dans laquelle le théologien, se mettant au niveau de l'homme charnel et même de l'homme résistant à Dieu, ne mettrait en ouevre qu'une partie de ses ressources, à savoir celles qui sont accessibles à un tel homme et *valables pour lui*." See Y. M. Congar, *La foi et la théologie*. Paris 1962. p. 184. The italics are mine.
34 See "East Asian Study Week on Mission Catechetics," *Lumen Vitae* XVII (1962), 723.
35 For a powerful modern effort of synthesis see J. Coppens, "Essai de synthèse apologétique," *Ephemerides theologicae Lovaniensis* 14 (1937), 447-66.
36 See Jean Guitton, *Jésus* (Paris 1957) and G. Lambert, "A Modern Presentation of Christ,"

Lumen Vitae XIII (1958), 77-99. There is now an excellent study of this apologetical approach by Enrique Neira, S.J., *Una lógica del Problema de Jesús*. Madrid 1962.
37 See, for instance, Guitton's basic book, *Le problème de Jésus. I Les fondements du témoignage chrétien*. Paris 1950.
38 See J. Thomas Tseng, O.F.M., *De Apologetica Methodo quae 'via empirica" audit*. Hong Kong 1960. M. Grand'Maison, S.J., *L'Eglise par elle même motif de crédibilité; comment les théologiens se sont servis de cet argument depuis le Concile du Vatican*. Rome 1961.
39 See A. M. Nebreda, S.J., "Conversion: Keystone of the Missionary Process," *Lumen Vitae* XVIII (1963), 670.

transcendent eminence? Grace is a gift, and we can never claim it as belonging to us. There is a good treatment of this by Blondel himself in *Theology Digest*.[40] He explains how everything in man is an expectation of the great revelation of God. Man is not, so to say, cut off because, after all, God has made us for himself.

Let me conclude with the statement of the Bangkok conference concerning positive apologetics. The reason the conference used the expression "positive apologetics" is precisely to show that there is, unfortunately, a "negative apologetics." If we think of positive apologetics as described at Bangkok, I do not believe anyone would object. For it is nothing but the whole effort of the Church trying to speak, to spell out the message in a language intelligible to the millions who wait for it.

> Positive apologetics proceeds from a true understanding and appreciation of whatever is good and acceptable in a man's culture. It consists in taking due consideration of the man with whom we speak, and in removing the personal concrete obstacles which prevent his ready acceptance of the kerygma.[41]

We stress, again, we are not talking about causality. We are in the area of conditions, but conditions that are essential.[42] A most urgent need today is a theological elaboration of the principles governing this initial approach to the nonbeliever.

---

40 M. Blondel, "Philosophy Fulfilled in Christianity," *Theology Digest* 11 (1963), 27-32.
41 "East Asian Study Week on Mission Catechetics," *Lumen Vitae* XVII (1962), 724-25.

42 A. M. Nebreda, S.J., "The Preparation of the Message," *Lumen Vitae* XVI (1961), 401-02.

Chapter four *From*
kerygma
to
pre-evangelization

At the International Study Week in Eichstätt, despite the rich and interesting themes discussed, most missionaries felt somewhat ill at ease. It seemed that the real problem had remained untouched. You could sense this in workshops and especially during informal discussions after papers. We kept repeating that our problem was not how to organize courses for Catholic children or Catholic adults, but how to lead nonbelievers to the faith.

This was precisely the main concern of the meeting in Bangkok: to go beyond the work of Eichstätt and try to answer the problem faced by missioners. Bangkok, I feel, opened a new era in missionary theology and catechetics. The emphasis now moves, not from catechetics to kerygma, but from kerygma, the dynamic aspect of the message, to serious theological study of the relation of human conditions to the divine message; that is, from kerygma to pre-evangelization.

Pre-evange-
lization,
main
concern of
pastoral
activity

As Bishop Carter stressed, whereas previous church councils were primarily concerned with the definition or the redefinition of truths. Vatican II sought more to re-establish contact with modern man, who seems to be drawing perilously close to thinking that religion is no longer a part of his scheme of values. The Council sought to reexamine and reopen relationships; human relationships between the Church and those outside her fold and inside the Church among believers themselves.[1]

In this perspective it is not hard to realize that the main task focuses on preparing the message,[2] which Bangkok considered the first stage of the kerygmatic approach: pre-evangelization.

Actually, this work of first conditioning the human ground before sowing the divine seed has always been done by the best missionaries and pastors. But too often, I fear, the task was performed almost pragmatically and with a sort of subconscious resentment for having to put up with a necessary evil. As long as the apostle stayed at that level, he could not regard himself as a full-fledged Christian missionary.

This is why I feel one of the most urgent needs of the Church today is to elaborate, on sound theological grounds, the meaning and role of pre-evangelization in transmitting the message. It must be made clear that the *terminus ad quem*—man existentially taken in his concrete cultural, socio-psychological conditions—is as much a part of the theology of preaching as the *terminus a quo* —the word of God in its creative dynamism. The personalistic approach, which is clearly a characteristic of contemporary theological renewal, is a fitting background for a deeper, more accurate grasp of our problem.[3]

To forestall misunderstanding, let me stress immediately that when we speak of *evangelization* which is preceded by and prepared for by *pre-evangelization*, we are referring to the second of the three stages of the kerygmatic approach as described by the Bangkok conference.

We are not talking about the whole missionary process, but merely the second stage within the process, whose content is, according to Bangkok, "a dynamic heralding of the core of God's Message."[4] This should dispel the misgivings of those persons who fear that words like *pre-evangelization* and *pre-mission* might suggest an activity preliminary to and somehow independent of the missionary process. No, pre-evangelization is an essential part of the integral transmission of the message. From it, it derives intelligibility. This is why I agree completely with A. Decourtray who says that "it should be strongly emphasized that there it is question of the first stage of a really authentic evangelization."[5]

Complexity of Christian existence

To clarify things I will repeat what I have already said at least schematically; namely, conversion and faith are among the most complicated phenomena.[6] In several of his books, especially in the *Christian Experience*, Jean Mouroux explains what it means to be a Christian in this experiential sense, or as he puts it, this "total personal" structure.[7] There are many elements and you cannot single out just one and say, "This is it"; it is a complex, a total reality.[8] But in this complex Christian existence becomes the meeting point of three major lines.

1 Emmett Carter, "Head and Heart," *America* 109 (1963), 40-43. See also J. Blomjous, "Les dimensions de la Mission," *Perspectives de Catholicité* 22 (1963), 185-90; 23 (1964), 51-58.
2 See A. M. Nebreda, S.J., "The Preparation of the Message," *Lumen Vitae* XVI (1961), 399-416.
3 See, for instance, A. H. Maltha, O.P., *Die neue Theologie*. Munich 1960.
4 See "East Asian Study Week on Mission Catechetics (Bangkok)," *Lumen Vitae* XVII (1962), 723.
5 "Qu'est-ce qu'évangéliser?" *Parole et Mission* 6 (1963), 390. It is also in this light that the entire problem should be considered when F. Dreyfus voices his misgivings about the use of the words *pré-kérygme* and *pré-évangélisation* in his article "Le kérygme est-il uniquement christologique?" in *L'annonce de l'évangile aujord'hui*, edited by A. M. Henry. Paris 1962. pp. 55-65. However, the point of view is more particular, restricted to the problem of whether or not the biblical idea of the living and creating God belongs within the kerygmatic core of Paul's teaching.
6 A. M. Nebreda, S.J., "Conversion: Key-stone of the Missionary Process," *Lumen Vitae* XVIII (1963), 661-78.
7 J. Mouroux, *Christian Experience*. New York 1954. p. 14.
8 *Ibid.*, pp. 15 ff.

The first comes downwards and is the line of divine grace. Scripture describes it with different names: revelation (Matthew 11:25), attraction of the Father (John 6:44-46, 66), enlightenment (John 1:9, 2 Corinthians 4:6), witness (1 John 5:10) and the like. This line is the most important element in Christianity. Moreover, it is a gift depending completely on the initiative of God, and as such it defies human penetration. The case of the other two lines, however, is different.

The second line moves upwards, so to speak, and is man's free response to God's invitation. Man, confronted by God's call, is free to say Yes or No. He must make a decision: acceptance or rejection.

The third line enters horizontally, as it were, into the heart of Christian existence. It too has different names: mission, message, exterior witness, word of God, evangelization; in a broad sense, preaching. These names convey the same idea: the exterior proclamation of the same life-giving reality—Christ as the Lord—to which the Father's grace attunes, invites, and attracts man interiorly.

God meeting man in revelation and man meeting God in faith are the main mysteries making up Christian existence. Yet these two mysteries need a meeting point where Christian faith takes its birth. God could have provided otherwise, but he who lovingly decided to need man decreed to use human means. St. Paul expresses this when he says that faith comes from hearing (Romans 10:17).

Against this background we can now see how pre-evangelization fits into the human means willed by God to transmit his message.

The role of pre-evange-lization in transmitting God's message

Here it is essential to remember that the controlling law on practically every level of pastoral theology is the law of Incarnation.[9] The law of Incarnation, I fear, is at the root of the division between Catholics and non-Catholics. Very often you will hear that some Protestant theologian

68

does not understand Mariology, or the role we give to the mother of God; or he has trouble with our concept of the Church. I think the reason for their difficulty is that they do not understand, in the Catholic sense, the meaning of the mystery of the Incarnation: namely, that God literally took flesh and became man. St. Paul spelled out the full implication of this guiding principle of Christianity, saying: Jesus, "though he was by nature God, did not consider being equal to God a thing to be clung to, but emptied himself, taking the nature of a slave and being made like unto men" (Philippians 2:6-7). Except for sin, he has gone through every experience of human suffering (Hebrews 4:15). This seems to me to be the touchstone for every phase of transmitting the message, especially the witness phase. We are to continue the witness of the "faithful witness," Jesus.

But let us see how this applies to the problem of transmitting the message. The Incarnation of the Son of God is continued daily in transmitting God's message, which seeks to provoke or deepen personal faith. The same Word of God wants to become man, flesh in an individual. It is the line of Incarnation prolonged and reaching beyond the frontiers of time and space to this individual or that individual. If in Christ the law of Incarnation extends to every human condition, we can expect the same thing in preaching.

God could have acted otherwise, as many Protestants seem to feel he has. He could have gone directly to man without any intermediary. He could have offered his powerful word in the heart of man to convert him. We see no difficulty in this at all. But we are not speaking about possibilities or theories. We are speaking about history; and historically God decided, in accordance with the law of Incarnation of which preaching is a part, to

9   F. X. Arnold, *Pour une Théologie de l'apostolat*. Paris 1961. pp. 76, 79, 83. See also Arnold, *Seelsorge aus der Mitte der Heilgeschichte*. Freiburg 1956. Part 1.

use human conditions as he did in the Incarnation of his Son. St. Paul expresses this in a classical way when he says, *fides ex auditu*, "faith comes from hearing," comes from the word (Romans 10:17).

Now by accepting the word, God has implicitly accepted all dynamism, all conditions that the human word carries with it. The human word is already a peculiar, concrete phenomenon. It supposes an *I* and a *Thou*. A bird might utter some sounds, but we don't call this utterance "word" in a true human sense.

Contemporary theology, drawing upon the data of philosophy and psychology of language,[10] employs more and more the interpersonal, dynamic, existential character of the word. The word has been well defined as "the action by which a person *addresses* himself and *expresses* himself to another person in view of a *communication*."[11] All those three aspects—interpellation, expression, and communication—point clearly to the interpersonal character of human words. They are then perfectly realized in the divine word which embodies Christian revelation.[12]

Let me illustrate. Imagine that a Chinese man comes to me. For twenty minutes he gives me a beautiful example of singing. I understand only sounds. (I can read Chinese but I cannot understand spoken Chinese—the pronunciation is different from Japanese.) After twenty minutes the man says in French or English to someone, "I have just given a message to Father." Then I would stop him. "You haven't given a message to me. You have not told me anything at all. You have spoken, but not to me." It is one thing to speak; another thing to be understood.

I fear this is what happens so often in the missions and even here. We go home sad and resigned, mumbling, "Well I have done my best, I have preached. It is up to them if they don't believe." But wait a minute. Have you preached to them? This is the problem. And mind you this is not a problem of linguistics alone. Many missionaries speak a foreign language properly, and yet their message goes miles over the heads of the people. Why? Because the basic element of understanding is deeper. It is at the level of mentality, at the level of sensibility. What I am saying here applies to any dialogue with another whether it be in the confessional, in preaching, in catechism, in conversation, anywhere. All are different forms of transmitting the message.

God, I repeat, could have acted otherwise, as he has sometimes done. Remember the miracle of Pentecost. On Pentecost, God, so to speak, bypassed his own normal laws. The apostle spoke in Aramaic and people immediately understood him in their own language. God has sometimes done this, and he still does it today. I know Japanese missionaries who speak pathetic Japanese; nobody understands them, and yet they make the most successful missionaries. Why is this? The answer is that they are holy men and God dispenses with the normal law.

But as for us, it would be arrogant and absurd to say, "Well since I am the ambassador of God, everyone has to listen to me." We are God's ambassadors, but never forget we are not a plenipotentiary for God. We very often take for granted that, since we carry God's word, all should listen to us. This is absurd. We will discuss this more in detail in the last chapter, because I think it is necessary to adopt the right attitude about a missionary.

Here we must realize that just because we are ambassadors of God, he does not allow us to dispense with the accepted rules of an ambassador. God himself adopted them when he decided to communicate with men through human means.

Now what is the first thing that an ambassador must do to prove that he is authentic? Many people might pose as

10 See, for instance, K. Buehler, *Sprachtheorie.* Jena 1934. G. Gusdorf, *La parole.* Paris 1956. C. Le Chevalier, *La confidence et la personne humaine.* Paris 1960.

11 R. Latourelle, S.J., "La révélation comme parole, témoignage et rencontre," *Gregorianum* 43 (1962), 40, 41-43.

12 *Ibid., Gregorianum* 43 (1962), 43-45.

ambassadors, so we should not feel insulted if our credentials are requested. That belongs essentially to our role.

This is precisely the problem. We are often obliged to prolong for months, even years, this process of convincing our audience (those who receive our embassy) that we are true ambassadors. To begin with, how can we hope that they will accept us as a missionary of Christ if they do not accept us even as men or women? The first type of prejudice one meets in a non-Christian audience or culture is that of questioning one's sincerity. They wonder if we are fanatics. As long as they remain at this stage, it is vain to hope that they will take us seriously as ambassadors. First of all, they must accept us as men; then they will accept us as God's messengers.

It can never be overstressed that this need to accredit ourselves as God's ambassadors is not just a methodological or psychological requirement. It belongs essentially to the dynamism of God's plan to present his word in human words, through human channels. The fact that we are bearers of a truly divine message doesn't dispense us from painstaking preparations. Neither does it justify our impatience if people are slow or reluctant to acknowledge our credentials.

We cannot forget that God himself decided to use human channels to convey his divine message. So long as men do not recognize us as true carriers of God's word, they ought not accept us. In fact, they are obliged to reject us. It would be idolatry to accept as God's messenger some newcomer because he is eloquent or says something new and interesting. This would be absurd. It certainly would not be Christian faith.

Thus far we have been considering missionary preaching, transmitting God's word, from the point of view of God coming to meet man. If we now look at things from the point of view of man answering the call of God, meeting him in faith, we will understand better the place and role of pre-evangelization in the missionary process.

Father Liégé, who has perhaps best studied the problem of evangelization, sees it doubly conditioned; first, *in an immediate way* by man's dispositions; second, *in a distant way* by the milieu.[13]

Concerning immediate conditioning, which will be further elaborated in the next section, Father Liégé writes: "It is the work of pre-evangelization—not absolutely distinct from evangelization—to work on human grounds to open them to the Message of the Gospel." A little further on he reminds us that "the task of pre-evangelization can be very slow, above all if prejudices against the Church check it."[14]

Speaking of the remote conditions, he says: "It is obvious that many human groups are in fact impenetrable to evangelization because of the inhumanity of their daily life which does not even give them the liberty of entertaining the religious hypothesis." This is why "the task of pre-evangelization cannot be dissociated from a collective fight for the transformation of social structures."[15] The chapter ends with a formula which seems to be a key to our subject: "What we have just noted regarding social structures, can also arise in the field of mental and cultural structures of certain human groups, although it concerns a lesser determinism and a less collective one. Pre-evangelization will then consist of a purging of the intellectual climate by a presence of Christian thought."[16]

I have stressed elsewhere[17] that if Father Liégé had included in this vision the phenomenon of a whole culture appearing and growing on the margin of Christianity— as is the case in Japan, for instance—he should have

13 P. A. Liégé, O.P., "Évangélisation"; in *Catholicisme*, edited by C. Jacquemet. Paris 1954. IV, col. 755-64.
14 *Ibid.*, IV, col. 761.
15 *Ibid.*
16 *Ibid.*, IV, col. 762. See also A. M. Henry, O.P., *Esquisse d'une Théologie de la Mission.*

Paris 1959. p. 10. "Obstacles" are here presented in a vigorous way.
17 See "The Preparation of the Message," *Lumen Vitae* XVI (1961), 401-03.

suppressed the qualification "although it concerns a lesser determinism and a less collective one." He is probably thinking mainly of situations in France, where the impermeability to evangelization arising from mental and cultural structures might be restricted to more or less minority groups within the cultural phenomenon. But, prescinding from a discussion of whether or not this reflects correctly the French situation, we cannot forget, while studying the problem of evangelization at large, that there are cases, like that of Japan, where not only the economic and social fields, but the whole culture, in the broadest sense of the word, has been hermetically sealed off from Christianity.[18]

*Pre-evange-
lization
in the
context
of faith*

In his tract on faith in the Summa written by a group of French Dominicans, Father Liégé has new enlightening insights for the problem we are discussing.[19] Faith is not something that appears all of a sudden, unexpectedly, without any sort of preparation. Faith has its own dynamism, its own process. This is to be expected if faith is to be a work of Incarnation in which God's word goes to meet man where he is and as he is.

Liégé speaks about antecedents, both objective and subjective, and conditions of faith.[20] This distinction clearly echoes the one we saw before between immediate and remote conditions of evangelization. As a matter of fact, the antecedents of faith correspond to the immediate conditions of evangelization, and the *conditionnements* to the remote conditions. *Antecedent*, in classical scholastic language, points to the realm of causes, where *conditions* are something necessary but not causal.

All antecedents seem to converge on a deepening of personal life whereby man is able to see within himself what can be holy in his own existence. An atmosphere of human truth is therefore indispensable. As long as man is not sincere or does not want to see squarely within him-

74

self, there is nothing to do because the essential element is not there. You have to wait patiently and try to help him until he decides to build up this sort of awakening or deepening of his personal life.

But, Father Liégé goes on to ask, "Is that deepening of personal life, in which we recognize the remote subjective antecedent of faith, within the power of every man?"[21] This brings up pointedly something touched upon in the previous chapter. We often take for granted that the problem of faith is an objective problem. "I explained things clearly; he is a free man, therefore he should have understood if he only wished." Things are not so simple. You have to take into consideration the concrete situation, the whole background of this man and all that it involves.

"It is evident," says Father Liégé, "that numerous social, economic and cultural conditions promote or hinder that deepening. It seems that many men of good will do not accept the Christian faith because of certain inhuman conditions of life, and this is true on a wider scale than ever before in our time of technical evolution."[22]

Here again Father Liégé is laying special emphasis on the obstacles to faith arising from social and economic conditions. We do not need to repeat what we stressed above concerning the handicap constituted by cultural structures. The final remark of Father Liégé regarding pre-evangelization applies to both conditions: "A double task demands our attention along with that of evangelization: to create an atmosphere of human truth in which people's attention is directed to what can be holy in their lives; therefore, the material conditions of life must be

18 See, for instance, Thomas Y. Tomon, "The Church and Japan"; in *The Church and the Nations,* edited by Adrian Hastings. New York 1959. pp. 136-62, especially pp. 143, 161-62.
19 See P. A. Liégé, O.P., "La Foi"; in *Initiation Théologique.* Paris 1952. II, 467-524.

20 *Ibid.,* II, 467 ff.
21 *Ibid.,* II, 485.
22 *Ibid.*

bettered."[23] It is easy to see, however, that in the case of cultural obstacles the perspective will have to be considerably broadened and the task of pre-evangelization will be much more difficult.

Always within the context of faith, the role of pre-evangelization must be viewed according to the disposition of an individual or a group to be converted. This is basic with regard to faith. Both viewpoints, the individual and the collective, are complementary and must be carefully kept in mind.

From an individual point of view we might distinguish, for convenience's sake, three types[24] of people: (1) The man who has never really heard the Good News of salvation in Christ. This can happen not only because of evident geographical reasons, but also because of certain psycho-sociological conditions.[25] (2) The man who has actually heard the Gospel, yet deliberately rejected it. Thank God we never know who this man is. Still the missioner must always remember that man is really free to refuse! (3) The man who heard the Gospel, "knows" it, keeps many of its prescriptions, but never realized— or does not realize any more—how the Gospel is something absolutely personal, new, radical, meant to change him at his very "heart."[26] We recall here our ideas in the first chapter. Indeed, it is easy to see that many Christians fall into this third category. They need a conversion; they also must be "evangelized" and "re-evangelized" again and again!

The papers presented at Bangkok had the individual in mind, especially when they spoke of pre-evangelization: "In this stage, we consider the *persons* as individuals, and not the community."[27] But, together with this, which we could call *direct* pre-evangelization, Bangkok stressed as well the need and importance of an *indirect* or collective pre-evangelization. "It is obvious, however, that we should take into account the influence of the environment on the individual. The apostle has not only to work on the individual but on the structure and on the mentality of the milieu which influences him."[28]

Conversion is indeed an absolutely personal reality. It is a change of a man's "heart" in the biblical sense of the word. But who can deny that there are groups or milieux closed to conversion? "This collective reality, mysterious but unquestionable, is something different from the total amount of individual realities."[29]

We can therefore distinguish again three types of milieux. The approach to indirect or collective pre-evangelization will differ accordingly. (1) There is a milieu which has never been able to accept the Gospel because it has never had the chance to really hear it. It never had the possibility of showing its dispositions to the message. (2) There is the milieu that heard the Gospel and rejected it. This is the tragic possibility spoken of by St. John in the prologue to his Gospel, "and his own did not receive him." (3) The milieu which did not accept the Gospel in its true divine dimension. It was just another reality among other realities, another religion among other religions. The milieu may even have reduced Christianity to just a name or an appearance. But so long as the true conversion was not achieved, this milieu remains in real need of evangelization.

By situating pre-evangelization within the two converging lines of God's word coming to meet men (transmission of the message) and man's heart answering to God's call (faith and conversion), we better understand

23 *Ibid.*
24 We are borrowing here many elements from the excellent article of A. Decourtray, "Qu'est-ce qu'évangéliser?" *Parole et Mission* 6 (1963), 379-95, especially pages 386-88.
25 For deeply pertinent insights into our problem, see the masterful chapter "Hors de l'Eglise, pas de salut"; in Ives M. J. Congar, O.J., *Vaste Monde, ma paroisse.* Paris 1959. pp. 110-83, especially pages 136-37.

26 See A. Decourtray, "Qu'est-ce qu'évangéliser?", *Parole et Mission* 6 (1963), 382-85.
27 A. M. Nebreda, S.J., "East Asian Study Week on Mission Catechetics (Bangkok), *Lumen Vitae* XVII (1962), 724.
28 *Ibid.*
29 A. Decourtray, "Qu'est-ce qu'évangéliser?", *Parole et Mission* 6 (1963), 387.

how the role of pre-evangelization falls clearly within the realm of condition. But we cannot forget that conditions can be absolutely indispensable! To ascertain the importance of and need for pre-evangelization in the missionary process, it will be worth while to study briefly its biblical foundations.

Now that we understand the role of pre-evangelization within the whole missionary process (both from the part of the message coming to man and the part of man answering the message in faith), we see that pre-evangelization does not *cause* anything. It is only a *condition*, but an essential one.

Let us begin by taking note of a few things about pre-evangelization from theological sources. We consider first the biblical foundation. Very often we hear that we should preach like St. Paul. I like this expression very much, but I am afraid that it is often uttered naively. Often it seems to take for granted that St. Paul preached only in a thoroughly kerygmatic fashion. My immediate reaction is to ask, "And how did St. Paul preach?" Many take for granted that St. Paul was a sort of revivalist who would appear on a street corner and shout, "Christ is the Lord," and "Christ crucified."

We cannot linger long on this problem, so let me refer you to an article I wrote for *Lumen Vitae* in 1961. There the question was studied, devoting special attention to recent Protestant biblical scholarship.[30] We felt that if the Protestants recognized this truth, the problem must be extremely significant. Because of Barthian influences, the Protestants have always been very reluctant to recognize any sort of pre-evangelization or preparation as such. For them this was to diminish God's majesty or the power of the divine word.

Father Grasso[31] goes right to the point, asking: Are we sure that the apostle always preached in a totally "keryg-

78

matical" fashion, particularly when he had to face pagan audiences? Now the first thing to note is that, practically speaking, we can reduce to two (or one and a half) the only recorded incidences where Paul preaches to a non-Jewish audience. This is unfortunate, but a fact. We have only the famous seventeenth chapter of the Acts of the Apostles, namely the sermon in Athens, and the beginning of a sermon at Lystra in the fourteenth chapter of the Acts of the Apostles. The latter began much like the one at Athens, but it was interrupted at the fourth verse. We recognize the same approach, but the outcome is different and rather unexpected.

In order to get to the bottom of this problem, I have surveyed a great deal of literature touching on it. There is a whole library of writing on the subject. My concern was especially missionary; and it is from the point of view of missionary theology that you can see the implications of the sermon at Athens.

Let us go immediately to the difficulty many people have. Often it is said: "Yes, Paul tried that way once, but he failed and then he went on to preach Christ and only Christ crucified," as he says in the first epistle to the Corinthians (1:21; 2:2). This is an easygoing, naive generalization without serious thought. I don't think that today any scholar, either Catholic or Protestant, will agree with such a generalization.

One leading Protestant scholar, Gärtner, a Scandinavian who wrote in English,[32] says that it is evident that this record is one of the leading traditions in the first presentation of the Christian message. Otherwise it would be impossible to explain why Luke, who usually chose the typical examples, so to speak, of St. Paul's preaching,

30 "The Preparation of the Message," *Lumen Vitae* XVI (1961), 399-416.
31 D. Grasso, "Il kerigma e la Predicazione," *Gregorianum* 41 (1960), 431.

32 G. Gärtner, *The Areopagus Speech and Natural Revelation*. Uppsala 1955.

would have retained this particular example if it had been tried, found ineffective, and rejected.[33]

As a matter of fact, internal harmony shows that Paul's discourses at Lystra (Acts 14:15-17) and at Athens (Acts 17:22-31) are clear echoes of the plan sketched in I Thessalonians 1:9-10 and Hebrews 5:11—6:2.[34] This is why Monsignor Cerfaux, having shown how in I Thessalonians 1:9-10 the apostle sums up the circumstances of his correspondents,[35] can conclude: "We have before us the outlines of the discourse of Pauline propaganda, which we can reconstruct with the aid of the two discourses to the Gentiles in the Acts (14:15-17; 17:23-31) and thanks to the beginning of the letter to the Romans (1:14-32; 3:21-26) and the first to the Corinthians (1:21)."[36]

We conclude therefore that Nauck is merely stating a solidly established fact when he writes: "The discourse in the Areopagus is a typical example of the missionary preaching which found its model in Judaeo-Greek missionary literature. Luke is one of the best witnesses to a great tradition."[37]

The alleged expressions of St. Paul about human wisdom, then, mean only that actually it did not fulfill its task, which was to lead man toward the knowledge of God. They do not mean that St. Paul radically rejected his views of Greek philosophy. If he later has severe words for philosophy, Monsignor Cerfaux comments, nevertheless in the first epistle to the Corinthians and in Romans he recognizes its mission; he emphasizes that philosophy, following its nature, could have and should have led men to God and thus prepared souls to receive the Gospel.[38]

Let it be stressed therefore that the discourse of the Areopagus represents a traditional current in the method of announcing the message to pagans. To quote Nauck again: "Luke takes part, unwittingly, in the transformation of the idea of God which discussion with the Greek theology brought into the Church. The historical value of the discourse in the Areopagus lies in the fact that it is one of the few great witnesses to the meeting of biblical thought with the Greek spirit in the missionary domain."[39]

Haenchen, the classical commentator of Acts, opens the way for further discussion when he writes: "This extraordinary vestige leaves us thoughtful. Christian preaching could no longer count upon certain presuppositions among its pagan hearers (which it had found among pagans influenced by Judaism) to make the Message accepted. That is why the discourse in the Aeropagus—as in Lystra—presents a new way of preaching (different from preaching to the Jews) to meet a completely different situation. Luke gives a specimen of a missionary program for pagans uninfluenced by Judaism."[40]

Now let us study the main features of this missionary approach and see what bearing they have on our contemporary situation.

Character-istics of the primitive pre-evange-lization

Wilckens defines this first stage of missionary preaching as "apologetics of approach"[41] and Schrenk calls it "threshold missionary preaching."[42] Let us examine its characteristics briefly.

In his study Schrenk makes some observations[43] that have a direct bearing on the purpose of our study. According to him the Acts preserve for us the approach taken

33 *Ibid.*, p. 52.
34 See Ulrich Wilckens, *Die Missionsreden der Apostelgeschichte*. Neukirchen Kreis Moers 1961. pp. 86-91.
35 L. Cerfaux, *Le Christ dans la Théologie de Saint Paul*. Second edition, Paris 1954. p. 17.
36 *Ibid.*, p. 18.
37 Wolfgang Nauck, "Die Tradition und Komposition der Areopagrede. Eine Motivgeschichtliche Untersuchung," *Zeitschrift für Theologie und Kirche* 53 (1956), 36. See also pp. 18, 24, 31, 33-35.
38 L. Cerfaux, *Le Christ dans la Théologie de Saint Paul*, pp. 192-93. See also A. Wikenhauser, *Die Apostelgeschichte*. Vol. V of Regensburger Neues Testament. Regensburg 1956. p. 211.

39 W. Nauck, "Die Tradition und Komposition der Aeropagrede," *Zeitschrift für Theologie und Kirche* 53 (1956), 46.
40 E. Haenchen, *Die Apostelgeschichte*. Vol. III of *Kritik-Exegetisches Kommentar über das Neue Testament begründet von H. A. W. Meyer*. Gottingen 1959. p. 467.
41 Ulrich Wilckens, *Die Missionsreden der Apostelgeschichte*. p. 87.
42 G. Schrenk, "Unchristliche Missionspredigt im ersten Jahrhundert" (1948); in *Studien zu Paulus*. Zurich 1954. p. 145.
43 *Ibid.*, especially pp. 144-48.

in preparing the way for the message in Paul's discourses at Lystra and at Athens. Commenting on this approach, Schrenk states: "The objective aim is the same at both places. We are shown how Paul when faced with pagans ignorant of revelation, whether simple or highly cultured, takes the actual situation of his listeners very carefully into account."[44]

What strikes us immediately is this *captatio benevolentiae,* [45] which leads him to begin from the standpoint of his audience. It is a simple, human, spontaneous thing, coming from the mind and heart.

Still within the psychological field there is something more here than a mere *captatio*. It is "catching the attention of the listeners by something drawn from their own cultural sphere. Starting from a point of mutual contact, showing respect for their poetic treasures, the missioner wants to obtain a hearing."[46] It is obvious, as Wikenhauser observes, that Paul, "like every missionary had to start from the ideas and convictions of his listeners."[47]

But there is something deeper yet. St. Paul goes so far as to recognize "the relative amount of truth to his listeners, so as to go ahead on a common ground, then giving them the full Christian truth. That is why the Stoic-sounding phrases in the discourse at the Aeropagus have a theist, not a pantheist, meaning in the context of the Acts. It was precisely an axiom for the Judaism of the Diaspora that the *one* God of the Greek philosophy (or the *one* Divine Being) was the God of the Old Testament Revelation."[48]

Schrenk has expressed this happily and vigorously: "But the objective method of this threshold missionary preaching is that it seeks to create an atmosphere of understanding, and does not fear to take the ground of the hearer as point of departure, treating with respect his fragmentary insights of truth."[49]

How long did this pre-evangelization last? We cannot say. One thing is certain: as was his practice, Luke merely sketches the plan of ideas and trend of thought in the discourse.[50] But the question, as well as that of the problem of content and method of proceeding at this point, does not seem to us to be of supreme importance. What is of importance is that we should adhere to these same characteristic principles.

Pre-evange-
lization
today

Let us now reverse our original question. Instead of asking how St. Paul preached in his time, let us ask how Paul, in the light of what he did above, would preach today. This seems to be a far more pertinent question. The former question, I fear, is somewhat irrelevant, because St. Paul's time was so different from ours.

In order to show that this change of perspective is not rhetorical, I am going to outline briefly the main differences that exist between our time and the time of St. Paul. These are not differences of a superficial nature. They are deep and they make pre-evangelization today far more necessary and difficult than in St. Paul's time.

Take the Gospel message, for instance. From the viewpoint of the nonbeliever, Christianity today lacks the novelty which, in spite of a thousand prejudices, fascinated the contemporaries of the apostles and their immediate successors. In apostolic times the Gospel message was something new and revolutionary. As such it met with opposition, yet the truly good men (recall Virgil's description of those souls in antiquity who yearned for liberation, yearned for something pure and noble) now

44 *Ibid.*, p. 145.
45 See Wilckens, *Die Missionsreden der Apostelgeschichte,* p. 87; Haenchen, *Die Apostelgeschichte,* p. 458.
46 Schrenk, *Studien zu Paulus,* p. 146.
47 A. Wikenhauser, *Die Apostelgeschichte.* p. 211.
48 *Ibid.*
49 Schrenk, *Studien zu Paulus,* p. 146.
50 See A. Wikenhauser, *Die Apostelgeschichte und ihr Geschichtswert.* Munster 1921. H. J.

Cadbury speaks of "an illustrative excerpt." See *The Acts of the Apostles.* Vol. I of *Beginnings of Christianity,* edited by K. Lake and H. J. Cadbury. London 1933. pp. 4-5. W. Nauck, "Die Tradition und Komposition der Aeropagrede. Eine Motivgeschichtlich Untersuchung," *Zeitschrift für Theologie und Kirche* 53 (1956), 18, 36.

suddenly saw that the message must be true, because it seemed to go against every human instinct. This was a novelty, nobody can deny that. Is it a novelty today?

After twenty centuries of history Christianity appears to the modern pagan as something old fashioned, obsolete, perhaps full of the glorious past, but fit mainly for a museum.[51] This is the problem we face in Japan. Though they show an external respect for the Church, very often they just mean: "Yes, of course, I admire that. We should certainly keep religion; it makes a fine museum piece." This is the way it is also regarded in Russia. It exists in many places as a glory for mankind—which, however, means nothing in our lives. Existentially it has nothing to do with us.

Prejudices against Christianity have always existed but those of today are of a special breed. You remember how strongly Tertullian felt about this point. "One condemned what one did not know," Tertullian said.[52] "You are talking about us but you don't know what we are." That was true. No one did know. Although today the pagans are as unfamiliar with the true nature of Christianity, it is precisely on these grounds that they attack us. They are convinced that they have so much evidence against us that there is no question.[53] Take, for instance, the works against the Christian missions by Panikkar in India. He is typical because he quotes nineteen centuries of Church history, in his own way, using it as a weapon to attack us. The same is true in Japan and other mission countries.

But look at the message from within, objectively. Here again is found a really remarkable difference. Modern Christianity shows a striking difference from early centuries. The manifest presence of the Holy Spirit with his palpable action and miracles created a kerygmatic atmosphere which made an apologetic and even a theological presentation almost needless.[54] The whole atmosphere was so clear that it spoke for itself. I am not so naive as to forget that there were cases as bad as now, even worse. We need only recall St. Paul's words in the Epistle to the Corinthians. Still nobody can deny that the entire atmosphere was more kerygmatic. To get an idea of the difference this made, let's suppose that the Christian population today were reduced to the fervent witness of those religious or lay people actually involved in the apostolate. Automatically our influence on the pagan world would go up 10, 20, even 100 per cent. There is no doubt of this.

The problem, especially in the Eastern countries, is precisely this image. "Christian? You mean that those are Christian countries?" the people say. "Places like Australia and South America, where you could have placed thirty or fifty countries the size of Japan but which would accept only a few or no Japanese immigrants during the post-war period when Japan suddenly had to feed seven million more people in a place smaller than California—are these Christian countries? And you give us, as the ideal solution, birth control!" How can one answer that? It is true that these are "Christian" countries. Yet when a missionary starts preaching in a kerygmatic way without previously preparing his audience, even a boy of fifteen is able to tell him, "Go to Washington and preach there. Go to all those South American countries and preach. Ask them how far Christianity influences legislators who establish Japanese immigration quotas."

I am well aware that extremely delicate and complicated political factors are involved, and I do not mean to oversimplify. But it is important to realize what image we create in the minds of contemporary non-Christians. We are very proud that we can count five hundred million Catholics in the world. Yet analyze their external Christian witness and you will begin to appreciate the nonbelievers' quandary. I don't want to deny that they will be

51 D. Grasso, "Il kerigma e la Predicazione," *Gregorianum* 41 (1960), 428.
52 *Apologeticum* 40. PL I, col. 478 ff.

53 Grasso, "Il kerigma e la Predicazione," *Gregorianum* 41 (1960), 428.
54 *Ibid.*, 41 (1960), 429.

saved; that they are much better than they look to the non-believer. But Christians should be somehow shining, and there is anything but "shine" in them.

As for the miracle of the Church, remember what we mentioned earlier in connection with Vatican Council I. It is true that the Church is a miracle, the greatest sign.[55] But this is not sufficient to offset the negative impression. The miracle is moral in character and hence does not impress a stranger so much, for his initial focus is inevitably set on the less supernatural aspects of the Church. The nonbeliever never sees the thousands of good priests; he sees only the one priest who may or may not be the witness he should be. It is unfair, but it is a fact. Scandals make good headlines. We know that there are scandals in the Church and there always will be. These are the things that immediately strike the outsider.

The reality of sin in the Church makes it difficult for those who judge her from the outside to see her holiness.[56] Such is the case when our best students dredge up from church history some fact with which to attack us. Far from denying any unpleasant facts, we accept everything and even give them more details, taking care to situate them in their correct context. But this is sometimes a difficult process. Often what you say has a different effect on the person who is sincere than on the one who is just trying to harass you. For, outside as he is, the only thing that impresses him is the organizational aspect of the Church, with all the difficulties and prejudices that this evokes for him.

What about the scandal of the division among Christians? I don't think that our former president of Sophia University in Tokyo exaggerated twenty-five years ago when he said to the German missiologist visiting Japan, "If Christianity had come to Japan the second time as it came the first time, unified, Japan would be Catholic today."[57] Father Heuvers is a sober and nonemotional Westphalian, famous for his dry humor. Thus when he said that he meant it. Japan as a country could have been won as thoroughly as were the Philippines, for Japan was yearning for something. The founders of the new Japan had to find a fitting ideology for the great nation they dreamed of. Following the lines of German idealistic philosophy (especially that of Kant, Hegel, Nietzsche), they invented a nationalistic creed which bore striking resemblance to Nazi philosophy. The whole idea of emperor *worship* finds little, if any, support in their tradition. Many foreigners forget that. The Japanese emperor had always been a wonderful symbol of the nation, which was always conceived of as a family. As head of the family he was admired and respected. It is enough to see the whole tradition from their literature, from their earliest poems. There you find, side by side with poems written by emperor, poems by peasants and all sorts of people. The emperor was (and is again today) a wonderful father among his people. Of course they had all sorts of myths about the origin of the nation; and these myths provided a base on which this new philosophy could build a sort of artificial nationalistic superstructure.

The fact was that the Japanese were yearning for something. The entire moral conception was patterned along Confucian lines, and it was made to rest upon the Constitution graciously given by the emperor to his people. As a result, when the American occupation cut away this Confucian background (extrinsic law as a basis of morality), the whole nation, and particularly the young generation, fell into a sort of moral vacuum, or rather a moral

55 Denzinger, *Enchiridion symbolorum*, No. 1794.
56 In spite of a definite betterment of public opinion in regard to the Catholic Church in recent years, due especially to the work and the person of Pope John, a series of stock phrases, sometimes a hundred years old and repeated systematically, has not ceased. This is the case in Japan, in order to burn into the people's hearts the caricature of an obscurantist church, the enemy of progress, liberty, and science; or of a capitalist church, bourgeois, imperialist, and colonialist. See examples in J. J. Spae, "The Religious Life of Japanese Catholics and non-Catholics. A National Inquiry," *Missionary Bulletin* 11 (1957), 549.
57 T. Ohm, *Asia Looks at Western Christianity*. Freiburg 1954. p. 54.

groping for a "new morality" which all too often has been alarming amorality.

Will the Church today be able to fill up this vacuum and restore to that great nation the best of its traditional human and moral values? The task is gigantic; and the role of pre-evangelization is going to be an extremely difficult one.

Another observation is in order, taken this time from the viewpoint of those who preach the message. Who does not see here yet a further difference between the time of the apostles and our own time? The preachers of today, even at the psychological level, are no longer filled with that personal conviction which contact with Christ gave to the first heralds of the Gospel.[58] Remember the emphatic expressions with which St. John opened his first epistle. This is not a trifle; it is something very important and tangible. You can see, even today, the drawing power of a saint who is on fire with Christ.

He can work miracles. Of course, the work of grace is always there. Still there is a connaturality in the way a saintly apostle presents the message as opposed to an ordinary apostle. It is an atmosphere of communion, like the process of osmosis. You come within this influence and something happens. If we compare the time of the apostles with today, then we see immediately the difference. Moreover we can never overlook the deeprooted feeling in Eastern countries that Christianity is a religion of the West, a foreign religion.[59]

I would like to end this consideration of the difference between St. Paul's time and ours with a final observation. St. Paul never attempted to prove God's existence. He took it for granted. As Wikenhauser writes, "It is self-evident."[60] He tried only to show God's essence; namely, what God is like. But no one questioned God's existence. If missionaries could start like that in Japan today, perhaps 70 or 90 per cent of all our problems would be different. This is precisely the first major problem for most of our students. How do we bring home to them the existence of God?

The same thing applies to liberation from sin. How can we speak about salvation, Savior, and things like that when there is no real consciousness of a need for salvation?[61] Where does one begin in places like Japan, where they tell you upon arrival that this is a place untouched by any morality in the sense of sin? You know the famous categories of Ruth Benedict by which she distinguishes between shame cultures and sin cultures. She brings out elements which seem to indicate that Japan and many other places are not sin cultures but shame cultures. There are things no one does because of taboos or sociological pressures, or because they are not proper or chic. But they do not seem to rise to the moral level. I would not go so far as to say that; for, when you actually meet man at his own level, you find that he is, after all, a religious man and a moral man. But for a message which is centered on salvation, you can see the amount of groundbreaking needed before you announce bluntly to such a culture, "I am going to present to you a message of salvation."

Conversion, break and fulfillment

Turning to the tradition of the Church, we can see that it has always kept alive faithful echoes of Paul's open approach at the Areopagus, so far as non-Christian cultures, philosophy, and religions are concerned.

The Bangkok Study Week on Mission Catechetics is the most recent witness to this ancient Catholic tradition, since it went so far as to consecrate the *anthropocentric*

58 O. Cullman, *Saint Pierre, disciple, apôtre, martyr.* Neuchâtel-Paris 1952. pp. 194-95. See also Grasso, "Il kerigma e la Predicazione," *Gregorianum* 41 (1960), 430-31.
59 This attitude is particularly evident in periods like ours, of strong renewal of nationalism. To estimate the force of prejudice during the prewar days in Japan, see A. M. Nebreda, S.J., "Cómo se convierte un Japonés. Una página de psicología religiosa contemporánea," *El Siglo de las Misiones* 40 (1953), 452-57.
60 Wikenhauser, *Die Apostelgeschichte.* p. 201.
61 Grasso, "Il kerigma e la Predicazione," *Gregorianum* 41 (1960), 434.

approach as the first contact with the nonbeliever; that is, to "take man as he is and where he is."[62] It has described positive apologetics, which makes up the main content of pre-evangelization, in the following significant way: "Positive apologetics proceeds from a true understanding and appreciation of whatever is good and acceptable in a man's culture."[63]

This is but an echo of the best tradition of the Church. Let us quote only a few passages from the last three popes. Especially interesting is the Instruction given by Pius XI to the apostolic delegate to Japan on June 26, 1936. It concerns the participation of Catholics in certain funeral, matrimonial, and patriotic ceremonies:

> Do not exert any zeal, do not try any argument to convince the people you are to evangelize that they should change their rites, customs and usages, unless these be openly contrary to religion and morals. Do not introduce to them our countries but the Faith, that Faith which does not reject nor hurt the rites and usages of each nation, but wants them to be kept and protected.[64]

It would be impossible to recall here the numerous documents in which Pius XII took up this theme, so dear to his heart. We need only recall his famous words to the Tenth International Congress of Historical Sciences:

> The Catholic Church does not identify herself with any culture: her essence forbids it. She is ready, though, to entertain relations with every culture. But in each of them she introduces the truth and grace of Jesus Christ, thus conferring upon them a deep stamp.[65]

The same line was clearly stressed by John XXIII.[66]

These are but the most recent instances of the true Catholic tradition. They reflect something which was keenly felt from the very beginning of the Church.[67] Christian existence—conversion and faith—is indeed a wonderful new phenomenon. It implies a definite break, a *discontinuity* which safeguards the transcendence and gratuity of salvation. But as Father Danielou has well emphasized in an enlightening article on kerygma in primitive Christianity,[68] there is as well an element of *continuity* since the God who has fully manifested himself in Jesus Christ is the only God, the Creator and the God of human conscience, as St. Paul had stressed.

The first Fathers were imbued with this conception in spite of their apologetic task, which often called for sharp criticism of the pagan attitudes. Justin is a classical example of this Christian openness. He proclaimed in an unmistakable way the superiority of Christian wisdom. But he showed also a keen understanding for those "Christian" values which were embodied in Greek culture as scattered fragments of the total and perfect truth. He can even affirm: "Christ is the only begotten son of God. He is the 'Logos' in whom the whole mankind takes part. Those who live according to the 'Logos,' even if they live a life of atheists as Socrates and Heraclitus, in fact are Christ's disciples."[69] Philosophy, as Justin understands it, was a *praeparatio evangelica* for the pagans in the same way that prophecy prepared the Gospel for the Jews. "The Greek philosophers," he says "succeed in dimly grasping the truth by means of these 'seeds of the logos' (*logoi spermatikoi*) received in themselves."[70] For him to be a disciple of Christ was to remain faithful to the good already existent in the pagan world.

62 See "East Asian Study Week on Mission Catechetics," *Lumen Vitae* XVII (1962), 723.
63 *Ibid.*, XVII (1962), 724.
64 *Acta Apostolicae Sedis* 28 (1936), 406-07. See J. M. Cirarda, "Valores de las culturas y de las religiones paganas," *Misiones Extranjeras* 6 (1958-59), 263-64.
65 *Acta Apostolicae Sedis* 47 (1955), 681. See also his first encyclical, *Summi Pontificatus,* AAS 31 (1939), 576 ff.; also AAS 36 (1944), 110 and the encyclical *Evangelii praecones*, AAS 43 (1951), 497 ff. See how Cardinal Gracias of Bombay commented on this theme in his opening and closing speeches to the Nimegue-Uden Study Week on Liturgy and the Missions, "Rythmes du Monde-Abbaye de St. André"; in

Missions et Liturgie. Paris 1960. pp. 23-35, 224-30. See also J. A. Otto, S.J., "Kirche und Kulturen," *Stimmen der Zeit* 137 (1940), 356 ff.
66 See for instance his discourse to the participants of the Second International Congress of Negro Writers and Artists, *Acta Apostolicae Sedis* 51 (1959), 260 and his encyclical *Princeps Pastorum*, AAS 51 (1959), 844 ff.
67 See, for instance, A. Seumois, O.M.I., *La Papauté et les Missions au cours des six premiers siècles*. Paris 1951.
68 J. Danielou, S.J., "Le kérygme selon le christianisme primitif"; in *L'annonce de l'évangile aujourd'hui*, edited by A. M. Henry. pp. 67-86.
69 *Apologia*, I. 46.
70 *Ibid.*, II, 13.

This same openness can also be seen in Irenaeus' keen insight into the religious development within mankind[71] and in Clement of Alexandria, who clearly perceived the intrinsic unity of all that was true in the world and the harmony between faith and reason. In preaching the gospel, Clement constantly banked on the good disposition of pagans as a point of departure, as Justin had done.

We need not discuss such men as St. Augustine among the Latin Fathers or Basil, John Chrysostom, Gregory of Nyssa, and Gregory of Nazianzus among the Greek Fathers. Their understanding of the non-Christian culture and the degree to which classical thought influenced their presentation of the Christian message is too well known to need any further development here.

Steffes, who reduces the apologetic approach of the first Christian centuries to five characteristics, expresses the second and third charactertisics in the following way:

Christian apologetics, intent to build up a synthesis between faith and knowledge . . . 2) uses up all the possibilities of contact offered to it and speaks mostly in the language of its time; 3) it acknowledges various truth moments (*Wahrheitsmomente*) in the non-Christian religion, morals and philosophy, as well as moral-religious capacities in the souls of men. It refuses therefore to see only impotence (*Ohnmacht*) and evil outside Christianity and in nature.[72]

This is what Father Congar means when he forcefully states that Christianity is not exclusive, but *inclusive* in regard to the other religions:

The mystery of God, realized in Christ and preached by St. Paul, comprises the whole of creation, which finds its effective meaning only in Christ. . . . The Fathers of the second, third, and fourth centuries elaborated the idea of a certain presence of the Word in pagan religions: a captive presence, as it were, that had to be freed by the Gospel, a debased and misrepresented presence, that had to be purified by Christ. And indeed everything insufficient or false or idolatrous in heathen religions in a way has got to die so that they may be, in their good elements, taken over by Jesus Christ and in him brought back to the Father. The essential thing is the dogmatic assertion of a certain relation of other religions to the absolute of Christianity, and in the end a restorableness of them to it.[73]

Paul Tillich is bearing witness to a true Christian tradition when he writes: "Mission is neither the attempt to save individual souls, nor an attempt to unite the world's religions. Mission is rather the attempt to transform the latent church, which is present in the world religions, in paganism, in Judaism, and humanism, into something new, namely, the new reality in Jesus as Christ."[74]

It is significant, as we pointed out in the preceding chapter, that a man like Kraemer, so zealous to stress the uniqueness of the Christian message even in an exclusive fashion in his book,[75] has then been led to modify his strict views of noncontinuity.[76] His more recent book goes even further to regain the balance between the two dialectical poles within Christianity: break and continuity, elaborating on the importance of dialogue.[77]

Christianity is not bound to destroy culture and religion, but to purify them and to strive to vivify their valid elements with a new reality. What we wrote about individuals can also be said of culture and religion.[78] The individual person should keep everything good, everything noble, everything acceptable, but in a radically new way. Psychologists, speaking about conversion, will tell you that it is like a new "constellation" in which all the elements are reorganized around a powerful new center. The meaning and orientation have been thoroughly modified, yet all the valid elements are there.

This is what we mean by break and fulfillment.

71   See J. P. Steffes, *Glaubensbegründung*. Mainz 1958. I, 42, 45.
72   *Ibid.*, I, 47.
73   Yves Congar, O.P., *The Wide World, My Parish*. New York 1961. pp. 30-31.
74   "The Theology of Missions," *Christianity and Crisis* 15 (1955), 35.
75   Hendrick Kraemer, *The Christian Message in a Non-Christian World*. New York 1938.

76   H. Kraemer, *Religion and the Christian Faith*. Philadelphia 1957.
77   H. Kraemer, *World Cultures and World Religions*. London 1960.
78   See A. M. Nebreda, S.J., "Conversion: Keystone of the Missionary Process," *Lumen Vitae* XVIII (1963), 677-78.

All too often the aspect of break has been onesidedly stressed in missiology. The aspect of fulfillment must also be carefully studied and duly stressed. It is precisely this point of departure that we call pre-evangelization. We must start with this approach, for if we go to the non-Christians and tell them to throw away what for centuries has been their only contact with God, the basis of their highest ideals, not only will they not listen to us, but—and this is worse—we will have acted contrary to God's plan of salvation for man.

It is indeed refreshing to see how the missionary experience and concern of the Church has helped recover an awareness of this lost basic element of Christian tradition.

Chapter five

Principles
of
pre-evangelization

W e have arrived at the point where it seems quite clear that pre-evangelization is imperative. It is not an approach that may or may not be appropriate under certain circumstances; it belongs within the message itself. We have pointed out that this was the normal approach in early Christianity, and that the first apologists used to speak of pagan wisdom as a kind of non-Jewish equivalent of the Old Testament. God spoke through them and Christ was the fulfillment.

Christianity is both a break and fulfillment: break in the sense that even those elements that are reassumed and ennobled in Christian existence must, nevertheless, be reorganized around a new center. This presupposes a crisis, which we call conversion. A study of Catholic missions bears this out.

Pre-evange-
lization
and the
history of
the missions

L et us take an example St. Francis Xavier, who evangelized India and other parts of Asia. Except in Japan he was everywhere a typical kerygmatic preacher. There he learned through painful experience that there are situations that cannot be dealt with in a purely kerygmatic fashion.[1] Consider the way he presented himself to the *daimyo* (feudal lord) of Yamaguchi. In his Spanish mentality he thought that poverty was something that concerned only himself. He learned differently, however, when he appeared in rags before the lord. In the Japan of that day one never dressed for the sake of oneself, but for the sake of the other. If you were poorly dressed, it was an insult to the other. The next time Xavier came before the *daimyo*, he came attired in the finest clothes which were available.[2] This incident inaugurated a type of pre-evangelization that received strong stress in the first days of the Japanese mission.

The same applies to the approach used by the Jesuits Ricci and Nobili.[3] Even a man like Arnold Toynbee, biased by syncretistic views as far as religion is concerned, notes that the attempt of these Jesuits in the Far East was the first case in history where Christianity had a tremendous chance of success.[4] It is indeed a mystery of providence that God allowed politics and narrow-mindedness to frustrate this opportunity to present Christianity freed from the accretions of Western civilization and culture. As Toynbee says, the Jesuit experience in China and India makes us hope that a similar situation will arise some day so that we may yet see Christianity genuinely accepted in a completely different culture.[5] Here again we come face to face with the delicate and difficult problem of pre-evangelization.

The case of Japan

We marvel at the far-reaching insight by which Father Valignano, the genial organizer of the Japanese missions, saw the need of pre-evangelization. An intelligent Italian and close friend of the Jesuit general Father Aquaviva, Valignano came to Japan three times as visitor of the general. He found a situation in Japan which is wholly modern. I have studied the records of the sixteenth century, which often read as a page of contemporary history.[6]

At that time the Jesuit provincial in Japan was Father Cabral, a Portuguese nobleman who had been converted in India and had become a Jesuit there. He was a saintly priest and in a way a successful missionary. Yet he had a number of strange ideas. He was convinced, for instance, that the Japanese should never be admitted to the priesthood because they were too proud. He personally saw to it that the first Jesuit Japanese martyr, St. Paul Miki, although he had finished his theological studies, did not die as a priest. Cabral would not let him be ordained, and he remained a scholastic of the Society of Jesus.

This was the situation in Japan when Father Valignano arrived there. He wisely consulted many people as carefully as possible, especially the Japanese Jesuits. Through these consultations he came to know the peculiar character of the Japanese mission. Valignano made a decision which is one of the most revolutionary in the history of the missions. In his *Il Cerimoniale* we have one of the most interesting cases of total adaptation in church history.[7] Valignano saw that the bonzes of the Zen sect were the most respected among the people. They had a genuine religious spirit. He decided that it would be good to imitate them, in externals, as much as possible. They set great store on ranks and offices, from the Great Abbot

1 H. Bernard-Maître, *Les Missions des origines au XVI siècle.* Paris 1956.
2 H. Bernard-Maître points out the flexibility of Xavier in abandoning his first approach when he realized that it was necessary to do so. See *Les Missions des origines au XVI siècle.* pp. 284-85.
3 Richard V. Lawlor, S.J., *The Basic Strategy of Matthew Ricci, S.J., in the Introduction of Christianity to China.* Rome 1951. Johannes Bettray, S.V.D. *Die Akkommodationsmethode des P. Matteo Ricci, S.J., in China.* Rome 1955.
4 In the Reith lectures, for instance, given over the BBC and published later as a book. See *The World and the West.* London 1953. pp. 63-65.

5 *Ibid.*, p. 65.
6 See Alejandro Valignano, *Sumario de las cosas de Japón (1583),* edited by José Luis Alvarez-Taladriz. Tokyo 1954. Also J. F. Schütte, S.J., *Alexandro Valignanos Ringen um die Missionsmethode in Japan Juli-Dezember 1574,* Rome 1944 and *Valignanos Missionsgrundsätze fur Japan,* Vols. I and II. Rome 1951 and 1958.
7 Alejandro Valignamo, *Il Cerimoniale per i missionari del Giappone,* edited by G. F. Schütte, S.J. Rome 1946.

down to the common monks. So Father Valignano proposed a similar system for the Jesuits. For example, the provincial appeared as a grand lord, as far as externals were concerned, and could not go out without the company of a certain number of gentlemen. News of this caused an uproar in Rome. Fortunately, however, the general defended his friend to the hilt. (We cannot here go into further details of the story.)

Let us move from these externals to the message to be transmitted. Here we come to something still more significant in our search.[8]

Distinguishing the different stages in the missionary approach

Many people seem to think of the first mission in Japan as a kind of kerygmatic tidal wave brought about by a combination of saintly missionaries and the great blessing of God. The results of that mission were indeed spectacular. According to the most skeptical writers Japan had, at the end of the sixteenth century—in less than fifty years of mission—more Catholics than are there today after one hundred years of mission. This is all the more striking because at that time there were no Sisters, while today there are almost five thousand Sisters in Japan. The Sisters are especially successful as far as baptisms are concerned. Their schools are usually the best places for conversions (particularly if we include the families of the students). Today we have about four hundred Brothers as well. While at the time of the first mission there were never more than sixty priests, compared to some eighteen hundred today. What accounts for the difference?

First of all, Japan has undergone a wave of secularism. It is interesting to note that at the very time when the West was moving toward secularism after the Renaissance, Japan was experiencing a quite similar process of secularization due to an entirely different series of factors. Today Japan is one of the most secularized, agnostic, atheistic societies in the whole world.[9] This makes Japan a very difficult mission, one of the most difficult perhaps in the entire Church.

In spite of extensive modern mission activity in Japan, we still do not yet have, I fear, the degree of insight into the problem of pre-evangelization as did those first missionaries who arrived there around the year 1575. After much study and experimentation these pioneers decided upon a system of instruction for the Japanese that was completely different from any method used by Jesuits in India, the Philippines, or the New World.[10] Their missionary approach constitutes, in my mind, the first example of what we today call pre-evangelization.

They divided the mission instruction into two main parts: the first *catecismos* and then *doctrinas*.[11] You might think of *catecismos* as the equivalent of our catechism. The word is the same, but the content refers to what we call pre-evangelization. *Doctrinas*, on the other hand, dealt with the explanation of the Christian mysteries. *Doctrina* is still the name for "catechism" in Spain today. The Spanish catechism is called *doctrina cristiana*.

If we analyze the *catecismos*, we see that it is an attempt to build on existing Japanese attitudes toward religion. Seeing how reasonable the Japanese were, the missionaries planned their first approach with a decided emphasis on the reasonableness of the faith. (Even St. Francis Xavier had been surprised to see how reasonable the Japanese were.[12] They were asking all the time, "Why?

8 We now possess an excellent study of this problem written by J. López-Gay, S.J., "La Preevangelización en los primeros años de la Misión del Japón," *Missionalia Hispanica* 19 (1962), 289-329.
9 J. Roggendorf, S.J., "La crise de la civilisation japonaise," *Bulletin des Missions* 23 (1949), 233-34; also "The Place of Religion in Modern Japan," *Japan Quarterly* 5 (1958), 21-29. For the students, see A. Nebreda, S.J., "L'étudiant japonais en face du problème religieux," *Etudes* 307 (1960), 361-70.

10 See for instance, L. Lopetegui, S.J., *El P. Acosta y las misiones*. Madrid 1952. pp. 314-15.
11 López-Gay, "La Preevangelización en los primeros años de la Misión del Japón," *Missionalia Hispanica* 19 (1962), 307 ff.
12 *Ibid.*, 19 (1962), 296-99. See also P. Peretti, S.J., *Mentalidad y cultura del pueblo japonés en las cartas de San Francisco Javier*. Madrid 1955.

Why?" and the saint was told that if he could prove that something was reasonable, the Japanese would accept it.[13]) Using this reasonableness as a point of departure, the pre-evangelization process designed by the missionaries then followed three major lines.

The first was that of *salvation*. Buddhism today, as then, is concerned with the idea of salvation.[14] By starting with explanations of the doctrine of salvation, the missionaries were assured of a hearing and of arousing interest. It is surprising to read that missionaries were frequently called by the feudal lords to explain Buddhism to them. It seems that they could explain it better than the bonzes themselves. The section on salvation ended by showing that the notion was present in all existing sects.[15] Thus the first section took the form of a positive explanation of the Japanese sects themselves. This explanation was followed by a criticism.

The second line of development dealt with *God the Creator*. The Christian concept of creation is indeed one of the most difficult to understand. In Japan it was totally unknown,[16] and it remains unknown to this very day.[17] Since it is the first dogma of the Christian creed and the foundation for our relations with God, the missionaries felt obliged to take up the idea of creation. They discussed it thoroughly in their pre-evangelization, linking it up with the concept of salvation, which was already familiar to the Japanese. For it is God the Creator who offered us (in his Son) the way of salvation.

The third line of development dealt with the *immortality of the soul*. The topic was also considered basic in preparing the Japanese for the Christian message. They had a different view on this concept because of their ideas on the transmigration of the soul.[18]

Since the missionaries were closely united, it was easy for Valignano to implement the proposed plan. It was universally followed throughout the country. This is how Valignano described the mission approach used:

Catechism, according to the diversity and capacity of the persons, is taught also in different ways, since the catechists handle those who are learned men and have certain knowledge about their sects in a different way than those who are ignorant and peasants. But what is usually observed is that to the pagans who come for the first time, in order to see what we teach in our law without deciding whether they wish to become Christians, we teach them three things: first, that there is no salvation in any sect of Japan; second, that there is only one God, Creator and generator of the world, who has given the law to men of what they must do for their salvation; third, that our souls are immortal and that after death there is another life in which those who knew God, the true God, and lived according to his law will be beatified by him forever; whereas those who did not know this God, nor live according to his law, will be forever condemned to pains and the torments of hell. With these three things the Japanese usually decide themselves whether they wish to go on to study the catechism and become Christians or not ... This way of proceeding, I think, seems to be the same that St. Paul used when he was teaching at the Areopagus in Athens, and which we gather he used every time he dealt with gentiles.[19]

The final statement of Valignano is remarkable in the light of the preceding chapter.

The founder of the Vietnamese mission

The same approach was used by Father Rhodes, the famous founder of the mission in Viet Nam. His catechism was republished in 1961 in a double edition, romanized Vietnamese and Latin, as it had been published three hundred years before by the Propaganda Fidei in Rome.[20] This catechism is a most interesting example of missionary

13 See references in López-Gay, "La Preevangelización en los primeros años de la Misión del Japón," *Missionalia Hispanica* 19 (1962), 297.
14 *Ibid.*, 19 (1962), 309.
15 *Ibid.*, 19 (1962), 300-02.
16 *Ibid.*, 19 (1962), 309.
17 *Ibid.*, 19 (1962), 303-05.
18 This appears forcefully in the article of Francisco Pérez Ruiz, S.J., "God Creator of All Things. Christian Dialogue with Buddhism,"
which will soon appear in *Monumenta Nipponica* and which the author has kindly shown to us.
19 López-Gay, "La Preevangelización en los primeros años de la Misión del Japón," *Missionalia Hispanica* 19 (1962), 309 ff.
20 Alexandre de Rhodes, S.J., *Catechismus pro iis qui volunt suscipere Baptismum in octo dies divisus.* (Réédité à l'occasion du Tricentenaire de la mort de l'Auteur avec introduction et notes par André Marillier, M.E.P.) Saigon 1961.

catechesis. It shows better than any argument that pre-evangelization (without the name, of course) was not only understood but practiced by the best missionaries. Father Rhodes converted thousands, and he was said to speak the language better than the natives. In enunciating his policy he says openly that he had to change much of what he had seen other missionaries do:

> I thought it good not to attack openly the superstitions of the Tonkin sects before preparing for that decisive battle by reviewing some truth accessible to the natural light of the spirit: on the origin of the world, what ultimate purpose the architect of the universe had allotted to His creatures, and especially to creatures with reason, and with how many bonds He has attached them forever to His service. Such preliminaries lay in the soul a solid foundation upon which it is then easy to build the edifice of faith. At the same time one avoids causing embarrassment and shame in the hearers by frontally attacking their religious practices, and irritating them (which is no unusual thing), rather than rendering them receptive to our teaching. And actually, if we are to believe the outcome at any rate, having a care to dispose the audience favorably towards the Creator has given me very happy results.[21]

Following this method, Father Rhodes personally baptized thousands and laid a solid foundation for the mission.

The Bangkok Study Week has recovered, at last, this tradition and clearly enunciated the principles of pre-evangelization. Let us now take a closer look at the principles governing this first stage of pre-evangelization.

Leading principle: anthropocentric approach

When I proposed this approach for the first time at Eichstätt in 1960, some theologians were disturbed. To forestall any misunderstanding let me explain what I mean by it. I use the expression *anthropocentric* ("man-centered") in contrast to a Christocentric approach, which avowedly must characterize the presentation of the mysteries of Christianity in the later stages of the mission. I want to make it perfectly clear that the approach in pre-evangelization is radically different from the approach used in catechesis proper. The latter has as the only valid principle Christocentrism.[22]

Some discussion has taken place on whether catechesis should be theocentric or Christocentric. Frankly, I have never understood the point of these discussions. Do we know anything about God which Christ did not reveal? As St. John says so well, "No one has at any time seen God. The only-begotten Son, who is in the bosom of the Father, he has revealed him" (John 1:18). It seems to me, therefore, that the only way to be realistically theocentric is to be Christocentric. Why spend so much time discussing such topics as "whether-or"? Take the facts: Christ is the Redeemer, Christ is the fulfillment, Christ is the Light, the Way, the Life. If you see Christ, you see the Father, as Jesus told Philip.

This much is clear then: catechesis proper is not the stage where God adapts himself to man. It is the stage where man opens himself to God, saying "What do you wish me to do?" It is here where you see the importance of the break or crisis called conversion, which we spoke of earlier. If there is no real attitude of openness, the whole idea of catechesis is spoiled. It is a time when man must try with all his might and human skill to open himself to God. That is why the highest virtue at the level of catechesis proper is, as St. Paul put it, fidelity, faithfulness. "It is required . . . that a man be found trustworthy" (1 Corinthian 4:2).[23] Catechesis proper is a time when man tries to overcome his own narrowness and adapt himself to God. It is the start of the dynamic of faith, going out of oneself and attuning oneself to God's voice and grace. This is the time for the catechist to announce what God has done in Christ and continues to do through his Church

21 *Ibid.*, p. xxxiv.
22 See J. A. Jungmann, S.J., *Katechetik.* Vienna 1953. pp. 94-98. D. Grasso, S.J., "The Core of Missionary Preaching"; in *Teaching All Nations,* edited by J. Hofinger, S.J.. London 1961. pp. 54-57.
23 See P. Hitz, *L'annonce missionnaire de l'Évangile.* Paris 1954. pp. 54 ff.

—what God himself has revealed about himself in word, deed, and tradition, and what his plans are for the whole of mankind.

It is in contrast to this Christocentric approach that I say that pre-evangelization must be governed by an anthropocentric approach, in which we take man as he is and where he is. It is man himself who somehow leads us at this stage. Some people fear that a sharp distinction between pre-evangelization and evangelization, such as this, runs the risk of making pre-evangelization appear as an independent stage cut off from the whole missionary process. Yet, as the very word *pre-evangelization* suggests, it is only a *preparation* for the evangelization, dynamically inserted into and demanded by the logic of the message itself. We do not carry on pre-evangelization for the sake of pre-evangelization, but to prepare the way for Christ. That is why I insisted earlier on the theological aspect: pre-evangelization is not just theory, it is God's own way. It is the pedagogy of God. His divine "condescension," has set the pattern for us to follow and imitate.

In the stage of pre-evangelization we face men shut in by cultural prejudices, sociological ties, and psychological patterns. In such circumstances even human dialogue is difficult. So, quite naturally, our missionary approach must be different. Our job is to convey a message—and a message is essentially from someone to someone. A message means communication, conveying something meaningful. It follows that the preacher must, in truth, be the first believer. His belief, and his desire to share it with others, moves him to go out of himself, to sacrifice his own preferences, in order to see through the other's eyes and feel through the other's heart. His first goal is to establish a real human dialogue. This means he must take the other seriously. In doing this he is merely following God's example. It was God who first showed the way.

God takes us seriously, so tremendously seriously that he went so far as to create hell. Hell is the best confirmation of the fact that God wants to deal with man seriously. Hell is an alternative; God does not force his love on man. Man is free to love or not. It is a fact of human psychology that if someone does not want to love you, you can do nothing about it. God is simply there, gently inviting, calling, attracting, appealing, knocking at the door (Apocalypse 3:20). The first movement is pure goodness, initiative from God; but once God has given us the grace, it is up to us to decide to use it or not. The Council of Trent goes so far as to say that heaven is given to us as a salary (*merces*),[24] not as an alms. God makes it, so to say, almost a thing of justice, fully in the line of the Covenant, which is like a contract between two partners. Perhaps "justice" is not the right word here because, after all, the whole realm is grace; but once the first grace has been given, everything else flows normally. God is absolutely faithful in keeping his word. That is what I mean when I say that God takes man seriously.

If God has given us the example, what should we do? We must take our hearer seriously, his person, his conscience, his truths, even if they are fragmentary. He, in turn, will take us seriously; and in taking us seriously he will take seriously our message.

Here is the tremendous responsibility facing the missionary. God deigns to consider us the responsible transmitters of his message. If we fail, in a sense he fails. If we succeed, he succeeds. Now this is the point; if in our dealings with others we do not follow God's way of dealing with us, if we do not take people seriously, our work will suffer accordingly. For how can others see God in us if we do not mirror God in our actions? That our audience will not only hear us but also understand us, we must use an anthropocentric approach, which accepts man as he

24 Session VI, cap. 16, with the reference of St. Augustine, as well as canons 26 and 32 of the same session.

is and where he is. This approach alone will bridge the gap and make possible the dialogue.

In catechesis proper the virtue is, as we have seen, faithfulness to the message of God. In pre-evangelization the corresponding virtue is sympathy and understanding, whose main characteristics are patience, love, and especially a sincere desire to accept whatever is true and good in the lives of those who are to be evangelized. Only an attitude inspired by the Pauline exhortation in the letter to the Philippians will work the miracle: "Whatever things are true, whatever honorable, whatever just, whatever holy, whatever lovable, whatever of good repute" (Philippians 4:8). This is how Christians are to think and to behave.

There are so many wonderful things about nonbelievers! But one must know them, which presupposes a thorough acquaintance with the culture, traditions, social structure, and mental habits of the people we wish to evangelize. Thus the aim of pre-evangelization is not systematic instruction or teaching, but rather the creation of a vital and personal contact, an atmosphere in which a truly human dialogue can take place.[25] In this dialogue we must discover what is closest to the heart of the other, what are his values and his convictions.

More than anything else, the procedure here will be to let him talk and ask questions. Through these questions we will learn about him, his person, his life. Very often men have more good in them than they themselves suspect or realize. Our dialogue will allow these good things to surface, and we will be able to show their true relation to the world of religion.

It is evident that in the stage of pre-evangelization psychology will have priority over logic in the matters to be touched upon. This holds true also with regard to the order and manner of proposing them.[26] Let me close this chapter with an example of pre-evangelization in action which illustrates better than many theoretical explanations what I mean by the anthropocentric approach as the guiding principle of initial contacts with an unbeliever.

I was on my way to Tokyo by train. Halfway through the trip, at Osaka, a man of about forty entered the compartment and with awkward shyness asked to take a seat in front of me.

At the time I was reading a Japanese magazine and saw that the man noticed this at once. A few more glances told me that this man would like to start a conversation, but did not dare to. After nervously smoking several cigarettes the man mustered his courage for a first question: "I see that you can read Japanese. It must have been quite a problem to learn our difficult language. How long have you been in this country?"

This question was the start of a conversation that prolonged itself for hours until he got off the train near Yokohama. Little by little, as the conversation progressed, I was able to form a picture of the man.

Shortly after our conversation began, the man said, "You are Catholic, aren't you? I know very little about Catholicism, only what people say about it in Japan: that you are severe and exacting. Take for instance your high school Eikô Gakuen. It has a tremendous reputation in our whole area. You have there quite a Spartan type of education . . ."

His remark, far from disapproving, seemed to carry an undertone of open admiration.

All of a sudden, as if remembering something, he said, "Oh yes, there is something I should like to ask you. In the company where I work as an engineer there was a responsible worker and a fine man. He was about to marry when he became seriously ill and had to be sent to a sanitarium. While he was recovering, another young engineer of our company, a friend of the sick man and a Catholic, started going out with the sick man's girl. Now he plans to marry her. What do you think about this?"

His eyes breathed fire. I parried the question, "How do you feel about it?"

"Well," he said, "as any decent man would, I feel that this is awful, horrible! It is robbery and indignity . . ."

It was midnight by now. While everyone in the train seemed to have fallen asleep, our conversation grew more and more ani-

25 See A. M. Nebreda, S.J., "El gran caos de la hora actual japonesa," *Hechos y Dichos* 32 (1956), 415-17.

26 A. M. Nebreda, S.J., *Distinguishing the Different Stages in Missionary Preaching*. Rome 1962. pp. 23-24.

mated. By his words and gestures this noble individual demonstrated a sense of duty and justice that one could wish for in every Christian. Listening to him, I could see that he was a man fully devoted to his family, his wife and two children.

After several hours I ventured a big question. "What do you think of religion?"

He stared at me for a while, but there was neither disgust nor surprise in his eyes. It seemed as though he had been expecting the question.

"Well, you see, I don't belong to any religion myself, but I respect religion sincerely. Last year when my two sons became seriously ill, a friend of ours, seeing how worried I was, insisted that I not call a doctor, but rather that I ask a famous healer to come in. I became angry and flatly refused. I respect religion, but I don't want things to be all mixed up. Science is one thing; religion is another. Religion is a different world, it belongs to the realm of the heart . . ."

I allowed him to talk for a long, long time. Without realizing it he was thus giving me a precious background which I could draw upon later. From his ideas about religion it was not difficult to recognize an extremely sound mind and, above all, a golden heart.

Dawn was beginning to break when I said to him with real conviction, "Believe me, you are not so far from what we Catholics are and think." And to his astonishment I went on: "What you find distasteful and repulsive in the religions you know is what we too dislike, because is it only a caricature of religion."

Then I began to talk to him about God, and how with fatherly care he rules over the destinies of the world—a world which he created out of love. I told him how God lets his voice be heard, quiet and low, but definitely clear through the voice of our own conscience. "Who taught you that the behavior of that young engineer was bad and the contrary good? Was it your teacher at school? Was it your mother?" The man listened intently, with his eyes closed, and nodded all the time. After all, I was simply explaining things he himself knew and experienced, although he had never reflected upon them before.

Then he said, visibly moved: "This is the first time that anyone has talked to me about religion like this. . . I had never looked at it in this way. I want to study Catholicism and see how it explains the mysteries of our life. I promise you that I will do so."

When later he got off the train at Yokohama, he turned three times to thank me for the conversation of the night.

Chapter six ***Pedagogy***
of
pre-evangelization

In the previous chapter we discussed the guiding principle of pre-evangelization; namely, that we must approach man anthropocentrically. In this chapter we will discuss two corollaries that flow from this guiding principle.

Personal,
individual
contact

The first corollary is that we must have some sort of personal, individual contact with the person to whom we wish to communicate the message. A dialogue is impossible in a crowd. We must remember that an adult listener has a rather mature personality and is not so malleable and adaptable as a child. Everything in him has attained a degree of differentiation from his associates which makes him an individual. He must be treated as such.[1]

This is why, generally speaking, group instruction in religious education is difficult unless the group is homogeneous or has already had some elementary catechesis.[2]

---

1   A. Chicot, "From Catechesis to the Catechumenate," *Lumen Vitae* XII (1957), 483-84.
2   *Ibid.*, XII (1957), 487.

If this is so of catechesis proper, it is even more so of pre-evangelization. Catechesis starts with a point of unity; all of them believe. They have all gone through an initial conversion. This gives them something in common. Pre-evangelization presents a problem in that the audience comes from all possible backgrounds and often has nothing in common. This is especially true at the moral level where conversion takes place.

Discernment of motives The first task in pre-evangelization is to discover the motives that have brought these people to us.[3] Since all are adults it is likely that many varied motives are at work. Some will come already converted—for example, Protestants who have already experienced conversion are, generally speaking, already prepared for the kerygma and even for catechesis. Still other people come to us who have undergone conversion because of a shock, some reading or some person. One has only to lead these to the heart of the mystery which they already seek and love.

Others, however, are still far from conversion. Here again they will have come because of a friend, a book, or an experience. Perhaps they have seen a death or other event that has given them a glimpse into the mystery.

Yet for others, and this is an important point, the occasion might be marriage to a Catholic. Here there is danger that adult baptism will be a mere formality.[4] That is why in France the official policy, at the moment, is never to subordinate baptism to matrimony. These are two different sacraments and it is evident that the sacrament of baptism is psychologically much more important than the sacrament of matrimony. Too often people want to be married in the Church and so will say, "All right, now I want to be instructed." But this is not a religious move. It is frequently only the desire to please a partner. No wonder that in France, for instance, an appalling number of adult converts used to fall away within a few months after baptism. This kind of situation, as we mentioned earlier, has brought on many recent developments in pastoral theology. The theologians have been literally forced by the painful experiences of pastors to face these facts. Why was it that 80 per cent of French adults systematically fell away? Evidently there had been no conversion.

Many people who come for instructions on this basis are ready to accept anything we want. I am reminded of one of the main characters in Evelyn Waugh's *Brideshead Revisited*.[5] Men have no difficulty at all with theoretical and formalistic acceptance; they just do not want their consciences to be touched. We find millions of people like this today.

There are still other types of people who come to us for instruction—the curious, for example. These come because they want to know something about Christianity. They may not have the slightest religious interest; they look upon a study of the Bible and religion as they do the study of folklore or a foreign culture.

In 1956 I gave a series of lectures, Introduction to the Bible, at Waseda University, one of the largest universities in Tokyo, some 25,000 students. It was a Newman Club project, and some sixty students came. I took for granted that everyone was Catholic. However, in the middle of the first lecture I saw from the radical, almost wild, questions that this was probably not the case. "Are these Catholics?" I wondered. After the lecture I asked the man in charge, and he said, "No, you are the only Catholic." My next question was why would sixty young Japanese come regularly to such a course for an hour and a half every

---

3   J. Letourneur, "Christian Initiation in France," *Lumen Vitae* XII (1957), 474. In this investigation of motives before anyone is admitted to the catechumenate, Father Letourneur sees one of the main improvements of the situation in France. See also P. A. Liégé, "Avant le Catéchuménat; la Mission," *Parole et Mission* 5 (1962), 23-32.

4   See for instance, what Father Coudreau has to say about this point in *Le Catéchuménat*. Paris 1961. pp. 20-21.
5   Boston 1946. It is highly enlightening to see the mentality with which Rex prepares to fulfill the "formality" needed for his marriage with Julie. Chapter 7, especially pages 192-94.

week. When I asked them, the most common answer was: "If you don't know something about the Bible, you are not a cultured man. Because it is impossible to understand Western history and culture without knowing something about the Bible." If I had said I was going to give them a course on Shakespeare or the *Iliad*, they would have come just as easily. Their interest was cultural, not religious.

In Japan we also have the person who comes because of what we call *giri*, which is an interesting sociological phenomenon. One cannot translate *giri* into any European language. It means a sort of sociological tie or obligation.[6] For example, a superior, a professor, or a friend makes a remark, which we would consider advice; but for the Japanese it becomes obligation. The professor might say, "Oh, by the way, next week there is a series of talks at that university which sound interesting." Immediately many students would feel obliged to go. It is important to be aware of this, because in the case of a relationship between a priest and a person being instructed, this sort of obligation can easily develop. If a person has been coming to instructions for three or four months, he has a growing sense that he owes us something. He might say: "I don't feel like being baptized, but poor Father! He has been so good to me. It has been three months, and I have taken so much of his time." This is a real danger.

Individual versus group instruction Let us now turn to the question of pre-evangelization in groups. I would like to begin by repeating what I wrote in 1961. I think it is still valid today, as far as Western countries go. I shall then add some careful corrections.

As a general policy, I shy away from group instruction when it comes to pre-evangelization. I must admit group instruction has certain advantages. It economizes on time, for example. It is also a great psychological help for people like the Japanese, who are instinctively shy in the face of an unfamiliar situation. For them the whole process becomes easier if they can feel somehow shrouded in a group atmosphere.

Again—and this is an important point to consider—group instruction offers an opportunity for progressive education in the Christian sense of community. Regarding this, there are often positive elements upon which we can build. For example, the Japanese people are much more community-minded than we are. This is especially discernible in young persons. To build on this sense of community would help protect them from the always recurrent danger of exaggerated individualism. It is sad to see how often Japanese people are forced to break with their native community and become individualistic, so that, by being individuals, they can become Catholics.

Group instruction, at least in the catechetical stage, could develop and foster a genuine community sense. For, as Christians, we can never go to God alone; we can never pray "Our Father" alone. Everything is bound up in that mystery of Christ which consists in sharing the very same divine life with others. We belong to the family of God; we are "children in the Son," as the Fathers used to say. These things remain too often mere theory. People enter our churches and feel "cold" because the worshippers do not seem to belong together. There is an air of solitariness rather than togetherness. Here the liturgical reform promises much help. It is important that people sing together, pray together, be together in order to understand that the kingdom of God is not merely an external organization. It is an organism, in which all are living members. From this point of view, I think group instruction has a very important role to play.

I feel, however, that this end can and should be achieved during catechesis proper, when people are beginning to

---

6 See the references in A. M. Nebreda, S.J., *Distinguishing the Different Stages in Missionary Preaching*. Rome 1962. p. 27.

share the same feelings. Catechesis is a time for a truly religious atmosphere, when the catechumen begins to breathe the pure happy air of the Christian community which will be his milieu for the future. The tone of those meetings should be more akin to that of a retreat than of a classroom. Many people are wondering, "Can I pray?" Everything must lead to an atmosphere of prayer. Otherwise, what is the meaning of catechetics? Only in prayer will the catechumen deepen that sense of Christ which is the aim of catechetical instruction. In a truly religious atmosphere he should begin to feel himself at home as he takes part in the worship of the Christian community.[7]

In instruction, therefore, the main emphasis should not be on exhaustive treatment, not on "How can I cover all these things?" At one of the Eichstätt workshops I remember how an experienced missionary candidly said that he couldn't see how we had time to give catechumens any of the Old Testament. Flooded with objections from all sides, he defended himself by saying, "There isn't time to say everything in the thirty hours or so that we have at our disposal; we have to leave something for the instruction after baptism." He meant that thirty hours more or less was the normal time devoted to pre-evangelization, evangelization, and catechesis. Well, when I hear something like that, I feel ill at ease. How can you set a timetable for God? How can you explain the New Testament, for example, unless you put it in the context of the Old Testament? You simply destroy the idea of salvation history.

I wish we would keep in mind St. Augustine's words concerning what the catechumen is supposed to believe before he can be baptized. We are impressed by the tremendous faith he should have. There is a good resumé in the third chapter of Jean Mouroux's book *Christian Experience*, with quotations from the Fathers about how the catechumens (who were fondly called "Christians") were supposed to be tested and proved before they could be baptized.[8] Faith was indispensable. Then and only then could the sacrament of baptism, called "the sacrament of faith," be administered.[9]

In the ritual of baptism we still have the question asked three times, "Do you believe in the Father . . . do you believe in the Son . . .?" And the person being baptized makes a solemn external profession. It is not enough that he believes interiorly; he has to show outwardly that this internal belief is something true.

When I returned to Japan last year, after five years' absence, I had a chance to contrast my ideas with those in the field. The experience led me to change my mind regarding the subject of group instruction. I see now that, in countries like Japan, it is not only advisable but almost imperative to conduct pre-evangelization in groups. The reason is, particularly, that *giri* which I mentioned earlier. If after coming to us for a while, the people under instruction feel tied to us, not for religious but sociological reasons, the very core of faith is in danger. It is important that we bring this home, especially in our schools. The core of any activity of the Church must be centered around true faith; that is, around *free* faith. Now if we endanger this freedom, this purity of faith, we endanger the very heart of what we hope to achieve.

In cases where a type of nonreligious pressure exists on an individual, we should leave the individual for some time in the gratifying anonymity of a group, where he can listen to us and examine us at his leisure.

This brings up another point that we should not forget. We think that pre-evangelization is a period when we examine people. No, it is a time when people examine us. I'm afraid that very often we fail all the way with our prospective catechumens. We say, "This is a tremendous

7 *Ibid.*, pp. 30-31. See also "Conversion: Keystone of the Missionary Process," *Lumen Vitae* XVIII (1963), 673-74.
8 J. Mouroux, *The Christian Experience*. New York 1954. pp. 48-60.

9 See St. Ambrose, *De spiritu sancto*, I, 3, 42 (PL 16, 743A) and St. Augustine, Ep. 98 Ad Bonifat. *Episc.*, c. 9s (PL 33, 364). Conc. Trid., Sess. VI, cap. 7.

crisis in the religious sense." In Japan less than 10 per cent of the catechumens persevere.[10] We may say that we gave the same thing to everyone and at least 10 per cent came through. But can we write off the other 90 per cent to the hazards of a free choice? Could it possibly be that we have failed with the 90 per cent because of our failings, whereas in the remaining 10 per cent God made up by a kind of miracle for our poor performance?

Yet after thus qualifying my position on group instruction and after allowing for cases such as the one in Japan, we have to add that some sort of personal, individual complement remains indispensable. Conversion and baptism are highly personal events. It is not the group that is converted; it is not the group which is baptized. Some kind of personal contact, guidance, and checking is needed. The group instructor must realize the importance of making himself available for individual contacts. Through these personal encounters the process of interiorization of the message is fostered and guided toward personal conversion and faith. Here we see, as the Conference of Bangkok pointed out,[11] the importance and need of Christian friends.[12] For the same reason the godparents-to-be should be carefully chosen and instructed in their important role of assisting the catechumen through the whole process from pre-evangelization to baptism.[13]

Witness,
core of
pre-evange-
lization

Now let us turn to the second corollary; witness. It is of prime importance. Witness is at the very heart of the transmission of the Christian message.[14]

We will begin by recalling a few points for background. We pointed out earlier that God decided to use human words to transmit his divine message. Through words God incarnates his Word in a man's heart.

Today we are, perhaps, more conscious than ever that a "word" is one of the most ambiguous things. In recent times, especially, we have been confronted with all kinds of ideologies in which beautiful words have been used to convey the most dreadful things. Daily we are bombarded with a flood of words; no wonder that we instinctively react to words with a kind of suspicion. As soon as we turn on television or radio, we hear that every tobacco or soup is advertised as "the best." We grow skeptical and hesitate to accept what we hear. We become, as it were, 'vaccinated' against the effects of words. That is why it is so wonderful to see that God, to prevent this danger, has taken due steps, in advance as it were. He decided that his message was to be transmitted through witnesses. Witness is not ambiguous. It reflects and expresses the whole man —the word of his existence. It is his living word, his life. Through the witness of Christians, God has decided to transmit his message.

The theology of witness

Now if we consider the whole theological issue, we see that God has always followed the same path. We know the Father because the Son was His witness. (John 3:11; 32-33; 16:25). We have never seen God. Only the Son of God, who was in the bosom of his Father from all eternity, has seen him and has revealed him to us (John 1:18). On the other hand, we know that Christ is the Son precisely because the Father gives testimony of him, "This

10 See *Distinguishing the Different Stages in Missionary Preaching*, pp. 19-20.

11 "East Asian Study Week on Mission Catechetics," *Lumen Vitae* XVII (1963), 723.

12 All the inquiries seem to agree on underlining the importance of personal contact with Catholic friends in the conversion of the Japanese. See, for instance, J. Shibutani, "The Statistical Study of the Converts in Japan," *Missionary Bulletin* 3 (1949), 24-27; J. P., "Converts Tell Why," *Missionary Bulletin* 6 (1952), 169-72; W. Kaschmitter, "Spark Plugs," *Missionary Bulletin* 9 (1955), 656 ff.

13 See F. Coudreau, *Le Catéchuménat*, p. 44. The book of M. Dujarier, *Le Parrainage des adultes aux trois premiers siècles de l'église* (Paris 1962) could be a rich source of inspiration. See also T. Maertens, *Histoire et pastorale du catéchuménat et du baptême*. Bruges 1962. pp. 137-46, 255-79.

14 For a more detailed exposition of this theme see A. M. Nebreda, S.J., "Role of Witness in Transmitting the Message"; in J. Hofinger and T. C. Stone, *Pastoral Catechetics*. New York 1964. pp. 67-86. The article appeared in a condensed form in *Theology Digest* XII (1964), 67-73.

is my Son, my beloved Son. Hear him" (Matthew 3:17; 17:5; John 12:28). We know the Holy Spirit through witness of the Son and the Father (John 15:26).

Witness, more than words, conveys a whole behavior which one might say "guarantees" the word. This is the witness that must be transmitted by the Church. As Christ transmits to the Church what he saw and heard from his Father (John 12:49-50), so she in her turn must transmit what she saw and heard from her Lord (John 17:18; 20:21). Just as the force of Christ's preaching resided in his works and personality more than in his words, so must this be the way of the Church.

We come to the same conclusion when we study the psychology of faith. Christianity is not a theory nor a series of truths. It is an ensemble of values, and values can be transmitted only through witness: "Value" is a concept different from "truth." The scholastics tell us that truth and value are the same thing—"verum et bonum convertuntur." Ontologically this is so. But is it so epistemologically, psychologically? I can think of many truths that mean nothing to me as values, whereas I can't think of a real value which is not true. For instance, two plus two are four. This is a fact, a truth. But I won't lose a second of sleep worrying about its implications. Likewise, there are other truths that leave me absolutely cold. On the contrary, when we speak about values, we always mean value *for someone*. This is something essentially incarnate. The personal, the subjective, is implied here. Even the man in the street understands that if we want to transmit values, it is idle to talk for hours and hours. To prove that this product is good and worth buying, just show that it works. This is what sells people ultimately.

Witness in the transmission of the message

So it is with Christianity: we can talk and talk, but unless we show that it works, our talking is of no avail. We must show what St. Augustine called the *appetibilitas*, the charm of the message. Unless we show why Christianity is called good news, and unless we ourselves are witness of this fact, our fellowmen will not be moved or believe.

It is essential that values—and values are the core of the message—be transmitted through witness. But the Christian message is not just a value but a particular set of values centered upon and summed up in a Person. Rather than the words of God, we believe the Word of God, who is a Person.

Now you cannot meet a person just by words; you cannot introduce a person as person through words or concepts. This can only be done by entering into the realm of personal relations—into a sort of instinctive, connatural, loving understanding. This is the only way people will be able to experience how good the Lord is.[15]

Christianity is revelation. But what is revelation? It is, as we saw, essentially God coming out of his own intimacy to tell us who he is—not what he is, but who he is.[16] We should never forget that. As soon as we begin therefore, even at the level of pre-evangelization—where the aim is to build a bridge for dialogue between human persons —witness is essential. It conveys to another that we are no longer in the realm of material things but in the realm of the interpersonal, where everything is mysterious.

We need always to remind ourselves and others that persons are not measurable entities that allow themselves to be enclosed in formulas and resolved in equations. Persons can be known only by revelation. We have no access to personal intimacy except through the free witness of the person. And persons never really witness to themselves except under the stress of love.[17]

If you look at Christianity from the point of view of its transmission and study Christ's missionary command, you

---

15 See especially what we said in Chapter 2, p. 25.
16 See the explanation in Chapter 1, p. 14.

17 R. Latourelle, S.J., "La révélation comme parole, témoignage, et rencontre," *Gregorianum* 43 (1962), 48-49.

see that it takes different forms. According to St. Mark, it is a message: "Go and preach the good news; the one who believes and is baptized will be saved" (Mark 16:15). For St. Matthew the idea is to make men disciples of Christ, not just to "teach" (Matthew 28:19). (Teaching for us carries a rather dry, intellectual connotation. For an Eastern mentality one could say "teach" because a teacher is like a spiritual father.) Finally, in the Acts preaching the Gospel is bearing witness: "You shall be my witnesses" (Acts 1:8).

These commands are not contradictory but complementary. We are supposed to transmit a message which leads people to Christ. But this is to be done through "witness." The embodiment of our preaching is precisely "witness."[18] No wonder, then, that witness is also at the core of pre-evangelization, the stage that paves the way for the message.

Let us examine this point more closely. When we consider that the preliminary obstacles to dialogue with a nonbeliever are not merely theoretical or intellectual, but rather total, existential prejudices that put us in a doubtful light as persons, then we understand that it is what we *are* much more than what we *say* that counts. This is especially true of pre-evangelization. The Japanese boy in front of me is convinced, through existential prejudice, that religion—and therefore Christianity—is simply ignorance, nonsense, insincerity, abnormality, fanaticism.[19] Now if he thinks that I am crazy, I will not prove by mere words that I am not. Those in a mental asylum are always convinced that they are sane.

The same can be said of a prejudice that questions our honesty or sincerity. Very often we find it hard to believe that people do seriously consider us insincere. And yet, it is very easy for them to do so. They compare us with any other employee. A Japanese boy will ask me very politely, "Who pays you?" I say "my friends" or "my family." "Ah, after all you are paid!" This is the way they reason. We appear in their eyes as a salesman who is paid to say that a certain kind of razor is the best. The fact that he says so does not prove that it is so. Maybe he himself does not believe it to be so. They apply this same logic to us. After all, we are missionaries; we have been sent to preach Christianity. This is our "mission" (they say, our "job"). It is normal that we should say that Christianity is the best religion, but this proves nothing.

Twofold aspect of witness

There is a dual aspect to witness. It has been beautifully described by Father Yves de Montcheuil, a French Jesuit theologian who was killed by the Nazis. The second chapter of his book *For Men of Action* concerns "witness," and shows how only witness, not propaganda, can be a real apostolate.[20]

According to Father De Montcheuil the difference between propaganda and apostolate is that the former does not hesitate to use methods or channels which in one way or another violate people's freedom. It is concerned only with results, not the means. The apostolate, on the contrary, esteems men and their free homage to God too much to use methods which, to acquire quantity, would spoil the very quality, the meaning, of dedication. And the only spiritual way of doing this is by witness, because witness respects the rules of free will and the Spirit working in man.

Father De Montcheuil sees our witness as continuation of Christ's witness. Jesus is the "great witness." In him are

18   See Yves de Montcheuil, S.J., *Problèmes de la vie spirituelle.* Paris 1945. pp. 21-47. J. Guitton, *Le Problème de Jésus.* I *Les fondements du témoignage chrétien.* Paris 1950. A. Retif, *Foi au Christ et mission.* Paris 1953. pp. 35-53 and 134-43. P. A. Liégé. "L'engagement dans l'éducation de la charité, "*Nouvelle Revue Théologique* 80 (1958), 253-63.

19   Father William Everett in his mimeographed course for our students at Sophia University lists as many as twenty of these typical associations which the word *religion* brings in Japan. See *Man and Religion.* Tokyo 1963. p. 51.
20   *For Men of Action.* South Bend 1963.

clearly seen the two elements that make up witness: first, transcendence; second, immanence.

Immanence of witness means that the Gospel Christ belongs to his milieu in such a way that he cannot be separated from it. He is a Jew, a perfect Jew. He eats like a Jew; he sleeps like a Jew; he thinks like a Jew. He is a perfect Jew, and even his enemies cannot deny this; he belongs essentially to his milieu.

Transcendence of Christ's witness means that this man, although perfectly a part of his milieu, is never reduced to it. Something in him keeps pointing to something beyond. There is in him an element that transcends the milieu. He is the way to the Father, he is himself God.

These two aspects must be true also of our witness. First of all, our witness must be immanent. We have to belong to our milieu in such a way that no one will question our authentic incarnation, in space and time, among the people we wish to evangelize. We must love our people and our time unreservedly. We must show our love for people in such a way that they can never question it.

I have seen in Japan that the last prejudice to go is this one; "Yes, but you are different." They do not mean this as an insult; they honestly think we have different blood, a different heart, different flesh. No, we belong to them; it is for them that we missionaries are there. I fear that, especially with religious, the questions of habit, of usage, of so-called "traditions" or externals badly impair our witness. We mean well, but if these things end up reducing us to the status of a man or woman from the moon, our missionary efforts are largely wasted.

This principle of the immanence of our witness should awaken in us the need for balanced and enlightened adaptation. I do not know why, for example, we should surround ourselves with mystery; we have nothing to hide. Let them approach us, see and examine us at their leisure. This is actually the thing that convinces our most difficult students. I have often experienced that precisely the students who are most antagonistic to us at the beginning are, after six months or so, the ones who come closer and eventually ask to be baptized. Why? Because they honestly "could not believe that we believed." They approached us with a challenging attitude. They questioned everything in us. They scrutinized our life. Then came the moment when suddenly they were confronted with our witness. They saw that we truly belong to them.

The second aspect, transcendence of witness, should guarantee that we are not reduced to the milieu. The importance of this aspect is too self-evident to need further elaboration; for if we are fully assimilated to the milieu so as to become just like the rest, then there is no hope that there is something special in us. Though important, this point has been, to my mind, too much stressed in modern missionary activity. We can never insist enough on this aspect of transcendence: sanctity in the spiritual life; but we should not do it in too exclusive a way. Both aspects, transcendence and immanence, are essential to Christian witness. In turn witness is essential to pre-evangelization.[21]

If the person with whom we are dealing is prejudiced, our words will not touch him. If we are a doubtful quantity, anything that comes from us will be suspect. The only way, then, to touch such a person is to wait patiently. The weight of our own personality must shine through sufficiently—through our words, and especially through our deeds—warmly enough to melt away all these prejudices. This takes time. This is also why witness is so essential in pre-evangelization.

Here we ought to touch on another point about witness. One reads often of the need for a *collective* witness. Of course, collective witness is the ideal if we have a com-

---

21 All the authors who deal with the problem of "precatechesis" have strongly emphasized this point. See, among others, P. J. van Hardenburg, "The Place and Function of the Catechumenate in Apostolate," *Lumen Vitae* XII (1957), 512; Chicot, *Lumen Vitae* XII (1957), 485-86; Letourneur, *Lumen Vitae* XII (1957), 475.

munity that shines sufficiently. But what about places where we cannot count on such a community? Let us be realistic. Take Japan, for instance. Where do we have the community that is going to influence the students? We must try to build it; but what about these boys in front of me who cannot be reached by it? If we do not have communities that are strong enough, bright enough, wide enough, to reach out sufficiently into the life of those who come to us for the first time, then it is *our* witness, our personal living witness to the faith, that must embody the witness of Christ.

Elements of witness

What elements should comprise our personal witness? It is not a question of teaching or instruction. It is a question of *being*. One is going to be analyzed thoroughly. Of all the elements of witness I would say that the first is patience. It is not easy to stand the daily strain of baffling differences. There are so many mortifying surprises that come of a different mentality. Even in so-called Christian countries the nonbeliever puzzles, almost exasperates us with his peculiar turn of mind. He questions things that we assume are evident and essential. Patience is also necessary because a mentality immersed in the prejudices of a lifetime can be approached only slowly—of course we would like to hurry.

To patience we should add love. Yet, just as patience alone is not sufficient, neither is love. This is a point I always stress. Indeed, love must always be the heart of the witness, the sign *par excellence* of the Christian message.[22] Yet there is a kind of "love" which insults him who receives it. Doubtlessly, it is offered sincerely, but sometimes the receiver regards it only as alms that it would debase him to accept. This is what we call paternalism. In this connection it might help to recall what Leo XIII, Pius XI, and Pius XII stressed concerning social justice. Charity can never substitute for justice. No, charity supposes justice and is added to it. Otherwise, far from being true Christian charity, it is a caricature. Perhaps the frequent disregard of this basic truth might explain why the word *charity* all too often carries along with it an unpleasant undertone.

What the popes say about social justice holds equally true for education, particularly for religious education. No amount of outward kindness will substitute for an earnest effort to appreciate and understand people, to see as they see. If we go on considering our students as "poor pagans," we may as well give up any hope to help them. Sometimes missionaries will say, "I have been in this country now for thirty, forty years"—not realizing that they have always been "looking down" at those "poor pagans," never making a serious effort to see them from within, to justify them. If we tried, we would be astonished to see how many things can and should be understood.

Love can be a very ambiguous term. If it is to be true love, it must be permeated with understanding. One of the leading Japanese missionaries, Father Sauveur Candau, liked to use the word *comprendre*—"prendre avec soi"; that is, "to take within oneself, without barriers, without limits, without pride, with intelligence, order, patience, and perseverance everything that might help towards the unity of mankind in Christ."[23] This calls for an effort of accepting people and trying to draw out from them everything that is positive. To arrive at this sort of charity, to be able to understand people, demands that we study them and the milieu in which they live. Only by doing this can we penetrate to the reasons for the various attitudes of unbelievers. Once we understand them, there will be no danger of paternalism or of arrogance.

22 P. A. Liégé, O.P., "La Foi"; in *Initiation Théologique*. Paris 1952. II, 482 ff.

23 S. Candau, "De l'apostolat dans les milieux intellectuels japonais," *Missionary Bulletin* 9 (1955), 178.

Years of personal faith and centuries of Christian culture make supernatural realities so familiar and normal to us that it is hard for us to fathom the psychology of nonbelievers. We must try to put ourselves inside the skin of those who cannot believe that we believe. I have often asked myself why I was born in Spain where, so to say, not to believe is almost impossible, and why this boy was born in Japan, where to believe is almost out of the question. Here we touch one of the most bewildering mysteries of divine providence. God is certainly not going to impute to them something for which they are not accountable. Thus, looking at things from within helps us to see them in their truer perspective. We see here that the ultimate reason for our understanding and the very heart of our witness must be reverential love, deriving from religious motives, because of God, in God.[24] Our witness must reflect the fullness of our Christian spirituality; it must reflect our sense of God. People must somehow feel that we *know* God, and that we think of God with deep humility, love, and reverence.[25]

Pedagogy and content of pre-evangelization

From what we have said so far it should not be difficult to understand what our tone and approach must be in pre-evangelization.

I do not wish, at this time, to go deeper into the pedagogy of this stage. Those who wish to study it more in detail should read Chapter III of Father Coudreau's book *Le Catéchuménat*,[26] in which he sketches masterfully the highlights of the journey through pre-evangelization.[27] The landmarks of such a journey are:

1 To welcome and to open
2 To understand and to prepare
3 To enlighten and to verify
4 To awaken and to guide

We find here a wealth of precious suggestions for conducting our dialogue of pre-evangelization. For dialogue it must be, even if this stage is performed in groups. Anyone will readily understand how difficult such a dialogue becomes when the instructor has to judge intuitively—perhaps from the expressionless face of an Oriental—the reactions of his listeners, their objections, their questions, their approval, or their rejection. This points up again the need for study of the socio-psychological context of the group or the individual facing us.[28]

As for the content of this stage, we need not repeat what we have already explained. Once we accept the anthropocentric approach as the guiding principle, anything could serve as the content of this dialogue.[29]

Father Coudreau outlines the following twelve themes[30] which could furnish material for a dialogue:

1 The "Good News"
2 God has entered history
3 The Church
4 Love
5 *Attente* (waiting, expectation) and the destiny of the world
6 Temporal values
7 Human freedom
8 Human misery, evil, pain

24 See A. M. Nebreda, S.J., *Distinguishing the Different Stages in Missionary Preaching.* pp. 33-34.

25 In the sense explained in the first chapter, page 15. See also A. M. Nebreda, S.J., "Role of Witness in Transmitting the Message"; in *Pastoral Catechetics,* edited by J. Hofinger and T. Stone. pp. 67-86. Summarized in *Theology Digest* XIII (1964), 72-73.

26 F. Coudreau, *Le Catéchuménat.* pp. 4-21.

27 It should be noted that what Coudreau develops here covers the stages both of pre-evangelization and evangelization or kerygma: it is part of the precatechumenate. Along the same line see "East Asian Study Week on Mission Catechetics," *Lumen Vitae* XVII (1963), 723.

28 See H. Carrier, *Psycho-Sociologie de L'Appartenance Religieuse.* Rome 1960. pp. 145-46.

This author stresses correctly the need of reaching the persons "in their context of social and cultural affinities," rather than the isolated individual, if the achieved attitude is to be stable. This points to the need of determining accurately those socio-psychological affinities in their negative and positive implications for the Christian message. Here lies the immense task of pre-evangelization.

29 See, for instance, what the Bangkok conference wrote in "East Asian Study Week on Mission Catechetics," *Lumen Vitae* XVII (1963), 723.

30 *Le Catéchuménat,* pp. 22-43. Keep in mind that Father Coudreau covers both these stages of pre-evangelization and kerygma (Note 27) to understand why certain of these themes are openly Christocentric.

9 God

10 The value of time

11 The smallness of the world and the immensity of the universe

12 Prayer

*Pre-evange-
lization
in action*

Rather than theorize further, let us now look at pre-evangelization in a concrete situation.[31] It will show clearly how the key to everything is the attitude that we embody in our witness. Pre-evangelization is not a question of theory; it is a matter of the heart, of sensibility, sense of God, sense of man. We should ask the Lord always to purify and refine us, so that we may never intrude as he never intrudes, never hurt as he never hurts, never force as he never forces. We must be there as he is, always to purify, to love and understand, to welcome.

Two years ago, in a lecture to students at our university in Tokyo, I discussed themes of pre-evangelization: the meaning of life, of death, and so forth. The next day I received a telephone call from a young student who wished to see me.

As soon as we sat down she said, without introduction and in a tremendously tense voice, "Why can't I kill my father?" You can well imagine my surprise. When she finally explained her situation, I realized that it was extraordinary.[32] Her father was incurably ill, and after fifteen years of illness he was growing restless and requested that his wife and only daughter hasten the end of his meaningless suffering.

This girl was challenging me. She was saying, "You talked yesterday about life and death. Now what do you say to this?" It was a delicate situation. The first impulse for a priest or any Christian would be to accept the challenge. Had I accepted it, however, everything probably would have gone wrong. Why? Because it would have reenforced her negative approach.

She challenged me, but there was something deeper behind her challenge than she herself realized. I had realized this, even if she didn't. There was something very good in her. Otherwise she would not have come to me. Her very coming showed that she was not so sure, so secure, in her attitude.

The second impulse—and here we touch the very core of pre-evangelization—would have been to use this occasion as a starting point for giving her a solid philosophical explanation of the meaning of life. But let us be honest. Do you think that you could have proved the wrongness of euthanasia (or of anything else) by arguing with a girl who was trembling in anguish as she was? This is not the time for teaching, for correcting, for instructing; it is the time for understanding, for keeping silent and asking our Lord to give you some of his compassion, his sense of the other. You must see the Lord standing there saying, "I have pity on these men and women who are like sheep without a shepherd."

While she talked I tried to encourage her, very non-committally, just letting her speak without introducing any hint of judgment or advice. Here the whole idea of indirect counseling is very valuable, provided that you bring to it a Christian spirituality; you cannot do this out of sheer psychology and methodology.[33] Nothing helps you to be humble so much as extreme situations such as these. In a case like this, what can you say? Nothing has any meaning.

So I kept encouraging her, letting her sense that I did not wish to inject my own ideas, that I wanted only to welcome her, to understand her from within—although I honestly realized that this was almost impossible. It took

31 See A. M. Nebreda, S.J., "L'accueil, phase décisive," *Perspectives de catholicité* 22 (1963), 83-91.
32 *Ibid.*, 22 (1963), 84.

33 See A. Godin, S.J., *La relation humaine dans le dialogue pastorale*. Paris-Bruges 1963. Also R. Hostie, *L'entretien pastoral*. Paris-Bruges 1963. Consult the bibliographical references.

less than half an hour before I could see a change in her eyes. She had come filled with resentment; now she was changed. Suddenly she started mumbling, "My mother and I, we see that this cannot be done." This was a complete reversal of attitude.

Again the impulse would be to rush in and say, "You see! You see yourself!" No, be quiet. Try to put yourself in her position and think, "If I were in her circumstances, if I had her mentality . . ."

The result of my listening and trying to understand was a change in the girl's attitude. In an hour or so she started crying like a child, and the whole problem came to the surface. The problem was not that she wanted to challenge me, nor that she was doubting. Her true plight was that of someone all alone in the face of the mystery of life, death, and pain. She did not see it as a mystery, but only as a puzzle. She resented it, hated it, and wanted to get rid of it. She came to me to prove to herself somehow that I was wrong. And since I had declined to accept the challenge, she eventually began to face again the lonely anguish so typical in today's world.[34] It is an anxiety that comes precisely from not knowing God, from feeling like an orphan in a world which man thinks he has mastered but which gradually seems to master him.

I tried honestly to assume her situation and her mentality. At one moment she said: "Father, you are thinking to yourself that if you were me, you would feel this way too. But what about you? What do *you* really think about my case? I want to know this." This point deserves special attention, for I am convinced that if we really try, spiritually and religiously, to understand someone as a person, sooner or later that person will try to understand us. So now she wanted to hear. I tried to resist a bit.

"You see, for me everything is different. I believe I understand your point. I try to think what I would do if I were in your shoes and faced with a situation like yours. I also have my own sorrows and difficulties; I am in anguish too, by many things I do not understand. But for me it is different because I believe firmly that behind everything is the hand of God, and behind the hand of God is always the heart of God."

Earlier she had said that she was an atheist, and now she was listening like a child. She had asked me my conviction, and now I could tell her. From pre-evangelization I was now invited to pass to the stage of kerygma; I was being invited to tell her who Christ was for me.

You cannot explain pain. The whole Old Testament is a most bewildering journey in the land of pain; pain baffled those men. The only solution they could think of was that it was punishment from God. Men still remained in this frame of mind in the time of Christ. When the disciples who had been three years with Jesus saw a blind man, they asked, "Master, who has sinned? Has he sinned or did his parents sin?" (John 9:1-2). The disciples could regard the blindness only as punishment for the sins of the individual or of his parents.

And what was Jesus' answer? "No, neither he nor his parents have sinned, but this is for the glory of God." The glory of God is that God is God and, as St. John said, "God is love." The glory of God then is the love of God. God's glory, his love, was never more beautifully or dramatically expressed than when Christ died on the cross. A philosopher can reason to the fact that God is good; but that God is so good as to send his own Son to die for man —this is beyond the human intellect. This is why in Christ we have the deepest manifestation of God's love, the highest expression of his glory.

If we analyze Christ's entire life, we see other instances that elude our human comprehension. Take the temple incident when Jesus was twelve. If you read St. Luke's

34 See, for instance, a sampling of testimonies on this critical situation of our time in *Man* *Alone. Alienation in Modern Society,* edited by Eric and Mary Josephson. New York 1963.

131

description, you cannot escape the fact that a great mystery lies here. The mystery seems to be not so much that Jesus remains in the temple, but that he remains there without telling his mother. When she asks, "Why did you do so? (not, "Why did you do that?" but "Why did you do so?"), Jesus does not answer her directly. There is no answer. He says, "Did you not know that I had to be in the house of my Father?"

We can only deduce that Jesus deliberately allowed his mother to suffer. To both Christians and non-Christians who cry out, "What did I do that God treats me like this?" Jesus' answer is to point to his mother and to his own heart. We can appreciate better Jesus' suffering, perhaps, because without shadow of sin himself, he freely accepted to "become sin" for us, to use St. Paul's strong expression, and to suffer. But what about his mother? Is there any "reason" why she should suffer? Here we are out of our own depth; we do not understand. Only the mystery of love accounts for the mystery of the cross. In Jesus and Mary the mystery of love is brought to its ultimate. If we try to understand things from within, we see not a puzzle, not a problem, but the mystery of a person, of a heart.

I frequently tell people in pain a story that happened when I was a Jesuit novice working in the children's ward of a hospital. One day I saw a scene that I shall never forget. There was a young doctor trying to give an intravenous injection to one of my little friends, a tiny, thin six-year-old. A woman was there too, evidently the child's mother. She was crying silently and holding the child. If a man from some other planet and not understanding human reactions happened upon this scene, he might have been tempted to shout indignantly: "What are you doing? You are torturing this little child, he cannot defend himself! Set him free!" And we, who know what a child is and what a mother is, would be tempted to shout back, "Don't you see how she is crying? Don't you see that she is doing what she is, not in spite of her love for her child, but just because she loves him?" It is the same with God. If he allows us to suffer, it is not in spite of his love but precisely because of it. Neither the child, however, nor anyone who does not know what human persons are, will understand. It will take time—perhaps ten years—but one day this child will know that thanks to the pain which he hated and resisted, he is alive today.

This is practically the only response we can make in the face of such a situation. We do not know everything; we do not know what is good; we do not know what is bad. We know that we are children, and one thing is clear: God exists. I can doubt about myself, but I cannot doubt about God. As Newman says, "I can doubt about my own existence." There are times when I walk as if in a dream and am not sure that I know myself; but whenever I think deeply, I find myself being confronted with God who must exist.

When we think of God, we must think of him as Father. This is our point of departure, and unless we stress this nothing is really clear. Now if you accept this (recall Christ's constant teaching on the matter), you need not always understand why this Father treats you, at times, as he does. We need only recall that there is a multitude of things we do not fully understand. When confronted with a difficult problem in mathematics or philosophy, we frequently confess that we do not understand. Faced with certain personal problems, we readily admit that we are bewildered. If we truly analyze ourselves in depth, we are forced to admit that we really do not know ourselves. Why should we be disturbed if we cannot always understand the actions of God? What depth of common sense is hidden in the expression of St. Teresa of Avila, "If I understood God, what a poor devil he would be!" ("Si le entendiera, ¡qué pobre Dios sería!").

We cannot look at the sun for even one minute, not because it is not there or because it is not bright, but precisely because it is too bright for our poor, weak eyes! The poor girl who came to challenge and harass me one day in Japan is today a Catholic. As a result of her problem and our conversation she began for the first time in her life to think seriously about Christianity, not as a puzzle or riddle, but as a mystery—the mystery of God who is a Father, who has a heart.

Index

Abstract terminology, 10, 13-14, 116-17
Alfaro, J., 9
Anthropocentric approach, 89-90, 92, 102-03, 104, 105-08, 127
Apologetics
  appreciation of, 47-48, 50-52, 62-63
  attitude in presenting, 59-60, 61
  catechesis and, 45-46
  for believers, 61, 62
  for nonbelievers, 50-52, 53-61, 62-64
  negative, 60, 64
  opposition to, 48-49, 54-56, 59-60
  positive, 63-64, 90
  Ramsauer on, 60-61
  Steffes on, 55-56, 59-60, 92
Aquaviva, Claude, s.j., 97
Areopagus, 80-81, 82, 90

Athanasius, St., 31
Atheists, 51-52, 60
Athens, 79-80
Aubert, R., 9
Augustine, St.
  baptism, 36, 114
  catechetical formula, 27, 44
  Church, 63
  faith, 10
  presentation of Christian message, 92, 118-19

Bangkok Study Week
  personalist approach, 76-77, 93
  positive apologetics, 64, 90
  pre-evangelization, 76-77, 90, 102
  purpose, 40, 43-44, 65

Baptism
  Augustine on, 36, 114
  faith, 3, 7-8, 114-15
  motives, 110-11
  Mouroux on, 114-15
  rite, 7, 8, 115
Barth, Karl, 47, 48
Basil, St., 92
Bellarmine, Robert Cardinal
  catechetical works, 27, 32
  faith, 8
  treatise on Church, 32
Benedict, Ruth, 89
Bernard, St., 62
Blondel, M., 63-64
Buber, Martin, 12
Buddhism, 17, 97-98, 100

Cabral, Francisco, s.j., 97
Candau, Sauveur, 125, 126
Carter, G. Emmett, 24, 66
Catechetics (Catechesis)
  adapted to times, 3, 9
  aims, 9, 103, 114
  apologetics, 45-46
  Bangkok Study Week, 43-44, 65
  Christological approach, 26-29, 102-04
  distinction between kerygma and, 41-42
  Eichstätt Study Week, 38-40, 42-43
  group instruction, 109-10, 113-14
  kerygmatic movement, 29, 38-44, 46-48
  missionary, 99-102
  religious atmosphere, 113-14
  role of witness, 121-26
  shifting emphasis, 11-12, 20, 29-38
  terminology, 42-43
  traditional, 26-29, 31-32, 88-92
Catechism
  anthropocentric-moralistic emphasis, 34-35
  Bellarmine's influence, 27, 32

Contarini, 36
Deharbe, 35
Dietenberger, 36
doctrinal emphasis, 29-30
German, 38
influence of Peter Canisius, 27, 30-31
new Japanese, 45-46
Roman, 27-29, 34, 36
Spanish, 99
Vietnamese, 101
Cerfaux, L., 80
Christian message
  contemporary attitudes, 84, 85
  dynamism of, 21-44
  in apostolic times, 83-84, 88
  preparing Japanese for, 88-89, 100-01, 115-16
  presentation in early Church, 24-29, 83-85, 91-92
  transmission, 66-67, 68-70, 72-73, 90-94, 100-01, 104, 105-06, 116-26
Christocentrism, 102-03
Clement of Alexandria, 92
Commandments, 6, 28-29
Communication, 70, 104, 106
Comte, Auguste, 21-22
Congar, Yves, o.p., 92-93
Contarini catechism, 36
Conversion
  adult, 2, 110-11
  aim of evangelization, 44
  break and fulfillment, 90, 93-94, 103
  complicated phenomenon, 67-68, 93-94
  personal reality, 76-77, 116
  reasons, 62, 110-11
Coudreau, F., 126-27
Council
  Orange, 7
  Trent, 3-4, 27, 105
  Vatican I, 63, 86
  Vatican II, 66
Counter Reformation, 3, 30
Creeds, 26-27, 28

Cyril of Alexandria, 31
Cyril of Jerusalem, 27

Danielou, J., s.j., 90-91
Decourtray, A., 67
Deductive method, 52-53
Deharbe, Joseph, s.j., 35
De la Taille, M., s.j., 18
De Letter, P., s.j., 16
Deschamps, Victor Cardinal, 63
Dialogue
    atmosphere, 54, 104, 106
    obstacles, 120
    personal contact, 109, 126-27
    themes, 54, 127-28
    with nonbelievers, 54, 62, 106-08, 120,
        126-34
Dietenberger, Johann, 36

Eichstätt Study Week, 38-40, 42, 65,
    102, 114
Einstein, Albert, 19
Enlightenment, Age of, 34-35, 37
Euthanasia, 128-34
Evangelization
    dynamic concept, 29
    Liégé on, 73
    meaning, 43-44, 66-67
    preparation, 66, 104
    terminology, 42
Existential philosophy, 12

Feligonde, G. de, o.s.b., 51
France, 40-41, 50, 74, 110-11
Francis Xavier, St., 95-96, 99

Gärtner, G., 79
German catechism, 38
Germany, 38, 51-52
Girault, R., 51
Giri, 112, 115
Godparents, 116
Greek Fathers, 92
Gregory of Nyssa, 92

Gregory of Nazianzen, 31, 92
Guitton, Jean, 62-63

Haenchen, E., 81
Harnack, Adolf, 25
Henry, A. M., 42
Hirscher, Johann Baptist, 37
Husserl, Edmund, 56

Incarnation
    abstract term, 10
    law of, 68-69
Irenaeus, 92
India, 22

Japan
    catechism revision, 45-46
    Christian image in, 85-88
    collective witness, 124
    cultural structures, 73-74, 87, 112
    emperor, 87
    missions, 47, 86-87, 95-98, 99-101
    nationalist creed, 87-88
    prejudice, 84, 122
    presentation of Christian message,
        88-89, 100-01, 115-16
    religious situation, 22, 87, 89, 97-99
    secularism, 98-99
    shame culture, 89
Japanese
    attitudes toward Christianity, 11-12,
        120-21
    impression given to, 59
    inductive thinkers, 53
    reasonableness, 99
    sense of community, 113
    sense of obligation (giri), 112, 115
    See also Nonbelievers
John, St.
    Epistle, 88
    knowing God, 18, 28, 103
    revelation, 103
    sin, 6
John XXIII, Pope, 90

John Chrysostom, St., 92
Jungmann, Josef A., s.j., 38
Justin, 62, 91

Kant, Immanuel, 33
Kerygmatic approach
  Bangkok Study Week, 43-44, 65
  beginnings, 38-44
  Eichstätt Study Week, 38-40
  preparation, 50-51
  Protestant churches, 47-48
  terminology, 41-42, 66-67, 99
  three stages, 66-67, 114
    See also Evangelization, Pre-evangelization
Kraemer, Hendrick, 47, 93

Le Guillou, M. J., o.p., 1
Leo XIII, Pope, 124-25
Liégé, P. A., o.p.
  catechesis and kerygma, 41
  evangelization, 30
  faith, 74-75
  pre-evangelization, 73, 75-76
Loew, J., o.p., 50
Luther, Martin, 31
Lystra, 79-80, 81

Marañón, Gregorio, 57-58
Marcel, Gabriel, 12, 24
Mary, 68-69, 132
Miki, St. Paul, 97
Milieu
  Christian, 2
  Christ's, 122
  materialistic, 38
  in pre-evangelization, 77, 122-23
Missionary approach
  anthropocentric, 89-90, 102-03, 104, 105-08
  apologetic, 45-46, 50-52, 54-55, 64, 90, 92
  Bangkok Study Week, 40, 43-44, 64, 65, 76-77, 89-90, 102

Christocentric, 102-04, 121-22
Eichstätt Study Week, 38-39, 65
in Japan, 88-89, 95-101, 115-16, 122
in Viet Nam, 101-02
kerygmatic movement, 38-42, 46-48, 66-67
relevance, 2-3, 20
St. Paul's, 79-83, 88
stages, 99-101
Tillich on, 93
transmitting the message, 70-72, 99-102, 119-20, 123-28
Montcheuil, Yves de, s.j., 121
Mouroux, J., 9-10, 114-15

Nauck, W., 80-81
Newman, John Henry Cardinal
  distinction between "reasonable" and "rational," 50
  faith, 10, 18
  prejudice, 56-57
Nobili, Robert de, s.j., 96
Nonbelievers
  anthropocentric approach, 89-90, 105-08
  apologetic approach, 50-52, 55-61, 62-64, 92
  attitudes toward, 53-54, 55-56, 58-59, 124-26, 128
  attitudes toward Christianity, 58-59, 72, 83-86, 89, 120-21
  dialogue with, 54, 62, 106-08, 120, 126-34
  methods of approach, 51-54, 58-59, 82, 106-08, 118-19, 120, 122-26
  need for Christian friends, 116
  obstacles to dialogue with, 120-21, 122-23
  personal contact, 106, 109, 116
  prejudice, 55-57, 72, 120-21, 122, 123, 124

Orange, Council of, 7
Orthodoxy, 8-9

Pain, 131-33
Panikkar, K. M., 84
Pascal, Blaise, 56
Paul, St.
  faith, 3, 6, 54, 68, 70, 103
  "in Christ," 6, 26
  Incarnation, 69
  missionary approach, 79-83, 88, 106
  mystery of Christ, 24
  preaching, 78-83, 88
Penance, 4-6
Personal relationships
  God and man, 5-6, 11-12, 15, 18, 19, 118-19
  persons, 13, 14-18, 19, 116, 119, 126-27
Personalist approach
  in conversion, 76-77, 116
  mystery of Christ, 24-26
  necessity, 9-10, 12-16, 66, 76, 109, 116, 126-27
Pentecost, 71
Peter Canisius, St., 27, 30-31
Phenomenology, 12
Pius XI, Pope, 90, 124-25
Pius XII, Pope, 90, 124-25
Preaching
  as communication, 70-71, 104-06
  divine message, 72, 104-06
  importance, 3
  law of Incarnation, 69-70
  missionary, 43, 66, 72, 80-83, 95, 104
  role of witness, 69, 120
  St. Paul's, 78-83, 88
Pre-evangelization
  anthropocentric approach, 89-90, 102-03, 104, 105-08
  apologetic approach, 50-52, 90, 92
  biblical foundation, 78-82
  Christocentric approach, 104, 121-22, 126
  conditions affecting contemporary, 83-89
  content, 127-28
  Coudreau on, 126-27

  group instruction, 112-13, 115-16, 126-27
  in context of faith, 74-75
  in Japan, 88-89, 95-101
  indirect, 76-77
  individual, 9-10, 76, 79, 116, 126
  length, 72, 73, 82-83, 114
  milieu, 77, 122-23
  pagan attitude, 83-86
  pedagogy, 109-34
  personal contact, 106, 109, 116
  preparation for evangelization, 66, 104
  primitive, 78-83, 88
  principles, 95-108
  role, 68-74, 94, 115-16
  witness as core of, 116-26
Prejudice
  against Christianity, 72, 84, 85-86, 120-21, 122
  against nonbelievers, 55-57
  nature, 56-57
Propaganda, 121
Protestants
  attitude toward faith, 8, 10
  division between Catholics and, 68-69
  kerygmatic approach questioned, 47
  law of Incarnation, 68-69
  prepared for kerygma, 110

Ramsauer, M., s.j., 60-61
Reformation, 8, 30
Revelation, 15, 117-18, 119
Rhodes, Alexander de, s.j., 101-02
Ricci, Matthew, s.j., 96
Roman Catechism (Catechismus Romanus), 27-29, 34, 36
Rostand, Jean, 24

Sacraments
  meeting with Christ, 5
  "mirabilia Dei," 28
  signs of faith, 2, 4, 7-8, 35-36

Salvation, 87, 89, 100
Scheler, Max, 15, 56
Schopenhauer, Arthur, 51
Schrenk, G., 81-82
Scripture
 foundation of pre-evangelization, 78-82
 grace, 68
 pain, 131-32
 Protestant scholarship, 78
 relationship of Old and New Testaments, 114
 study course, 111-12
Shestov, Lev, 12
Sincerity, 53-54
Sophia University, 86
Steffes, Johann, 54-56, 59, 92

Teresa of Avila, St., 133
Tertullian, 62, 84
Thivollier, A., 51
Thomas Aquinas, St.
 Creed, 28
 faith, 10
 sacraments, 36
Tillich, Paul, 12, 93
Toynbee, Arnold, 96
Trent, Council of, 3-4, 27, 105

Valignano, Alejandro, s.j., 96-98, 100-01
Van Caster, Marcel, s.j., 12
Vatican Council I, 63, 86
Vatican Council II, 66
Viet Nam, 101-02
Vries, Joseph de, s.j., 52

Waseda University, 111-12
Waugh, Evelyn, 111
Wessenberg, Ignaz Heinrich von, 34
Wikenhauser, A., 82, 88
Wilckens, Ulrich, 81
Witness
 attitude embodied in , 124-26, 128
 collective, 123-24
 contemporary Christian, 63, 85-86, 121-26
 continuation of Christ's, 121-22, 124
 dual aspect, 121-24
 elements of personal, 119, 124-26
 immanence, 122, 123
 propaganda and, 121
 role, 69, 116-21
 theology, 117-18
 transcendence, 122, 123

Zen Buddhists, 17, 97-98

About this book

William Nicoll of EDIT, INC., designed
Kerygma in Crisis? It was set by
SERVICE TYPOGRAPHERS, INC., Indianapolis, Indiana.
The text is 11/13 Janson;
the footnotes 6/8 Times Roman;
and the chapter titles 24 Janson italic.
The book was printed by PHOTOPRESS, INC.
on S. D. WARREN's 60-pound English Finish paper and
bound by A. C. ENGDAHL AND COMPANY, INC.,
in BANCROFT's Arrestox 60910.